Passive Income Ideas 2020

The Best Strategies and Secrets to Make Money from Home and Reach Financial Freedom - Amazon FBA, Dropshipping, Affiliate Marketing, Kindle Publishing, Blogging and More

© **Copyright 2019 by Jim Cloud- All rights reserved.**

The content contained within this book may not be reproduced, duplicated or transmitted without direct written permission from the author or the publisher.

Under no circumstances will any blame or legal responsibility be held against the publisher, or author, for any damages, reparation, or monetary loss due to the information contained within this book. Either directly or indirectly.

Legal Notice:

This book is copyright protected. This book is only for personal use. You cannot amend, distribute, sell, use, quote or paraphrase any part, or the content within this book, without the consent of the author or publisher.

Disclaimer Notice:

Please note the information contained within this document is for educational and entertainment purposes only. All effort has been executed to present accurate, up to date, and reliable, complete information. No warranties of any kind are declared or implied. Readers acknowledge that the author is not engaging in the rendering of legal, financial, medical or professional advice. The content within this book has been derived from various sources. Please consult a licensed professional before attempting any techniques outlined in this book.

By reading this document, the reader agrees that under no circumstances is the author responsible for any losses, direct or indirect, which are incurred as a result of the information contained within this document, including, but not limited to, — errors, omissions, or inaccuracies.

Table of Contents

Introduction 1

    What is Passive Income? 2

Chapter 1: The Right Mind for Your Business 8

    Take Responsibility 14

        Looking Ahead 16

Chapter 2: Dropshipping 19

    Starting Your Own Dropshipping Business. 23

        Where To From Here? 31

Chapter 3: Amazon FBA 34

    Building Your Amazon FBA Business 37

    A Few Extra Tips 44

Chapter 4: Affiliate Marketing 46

    Creating an Affiliate Marketing Scheme ... 49

        Promoting Your Offers 57

Chapter 5: Blogging 60

Your Own Blog Site 63

Building Your Blog 66

Chapter 6: Kindle Publishing 72

Where to Begin 74

Moving Even Further 80

Chapter 7: Social Media Marketing ... 84

How Do I Start My Own Brand? 85

A Few Tips Of Note 91

Chapter 8: Rental Income 95

Renting Out Your Property 96

Rental Structure 101

Chapter 9: Cryptocurrency 105

Investing In Cryptocurrency 107

A Bit Of A Heads Up 111

Chapter 10: Google Adsense 114

Using Google Adsense To Make You Money 116

Optimizing The Ad Experience 119

Chapter 11: Online Courses **122**

Creating Your Own Online Courses 124

Selling And Marketing Your Course..... 128

Chapter 12: AirBnB Business **132**

Setting Up An AirBnB 134

Your Airbnb Profile 137

Chapter 13: Dividend Investments ... **141**

Investing In Dividend Stocks 143

A Few Suggestions 148

Chapter 14: Forex Trading **151**

Trading in Forex...153

Trading Successfully 156

Chapter 15: Swing Trading **160**

Swing Trading As Income 162

Setting Up For the Rewards 165

Chapter 16: Personal Brand **169**

Creating Your Own Personal Brand 171

Monetizing Your Personal Brand 175

Chapter 17: Mobile App Development 178

Creating Your First App 179

Marketing And Promotion 187

Chapter 18: YouTube Videos 190

Starting Your Own YouTube Channel 192

Things You Need To Consider 199

Chapter 19: Photography 202

Creating Your Passive Income With Photography 203

Taking Your Photography Further 207

Chapter 20: Mistakes to Avoid 210

The Trap of the Mind's Impulse 211

Conclusion 215

Introduction

Money. We all need it to live in this modern day world. How much importance you attach to it is your own concern. However, it can't be denied that money can improve our quality of life and standard of living. Otherwise, why do we get up and go to work every day? For fun? Maybe. For the majority of us, work is a means to survival, and to a better life. It brings us the comfort of steady income. However, for most of us, a steady paying job is not enough for us to achieve our lifelong goals and live out our dreams. It may not even provide the financial stability that you need.

What are the solutions? Should we take on another job? Maybe you can. Maybe you have. Maybe your job is too straining, and the additional load will be too much. There may not be enough hours in the day for you to be in a position to do something like this.

This is where passive income can play an important role in your life. Irrespective of your circumstances, or your financial status, obtaining a passive income can drive you to greater heights financially, giving you more economic freedom and the platform with which you can achieve your goals.

What is Passive Income?

Currently, if you're employed, you are earning an active income. An active income is any income where you are required to have a direct and continuous involvement in the generation of income. If you don't go to work, you probably don't make any money for that day. That is the basis of active income.

Passive income, on the other hand, is the money that you can earn with minimal and indirect upkeep. With time, passive income can generate regular and sustainable income that will build over time. Besides, of course, the fact that you are bringing in more money, there are many benefits to acquiring a passive income (Wanderlust Worker, 2019).

For one, I'm sure you'll be aware that the increased income will give you a much more stress-free environment. You may find yourself deep in debt to pay your bills and fearing future outcomes. Here, you will find passive income will help to lessen your fears as you have will always have a backup solution; a viable option to fall back on should you find yourself in a crisis. You'll have more energy to invest in your days ahead, free from the what-ifs and thoughts of financial collapse.

With this, we can see another one of the many benefits of passive income: freedom. Given that you are not active in the work you are pursuing, this will give you something truly valuable in life, that many of us take for granted: time. You will have the time to do the things that you find enjoyable. If you're a parent, you'll have more valuable time to spend with your kids, giving them the attention that you may not have been able to before.

Maybe, like me, you have a desire to see the world in all its beauty, and with a passive income, you have the benefit of being able to be anywhere in the world, and still have the ability to work on your income from there. In our day to day lives, we probably plan a holiday way in advance, and then have to wait several more years before we have the ability to plan the next one. With a reliable passive income, you can transcend these boundaries, and travel however much it suits you. Remember that word: freedom. Freedom to do the things we love, with the people we love, and engage in all of the enjoyment that life has to offer.

With that being said, if there are all these lovely benefits stuff centered around passive income, why have you not heard much about it? Well, the truth is, you probably have, but maybe you weren't paying enough attention at the time. In the other sense, that it doesn't look to be popular, is that there appears to be several rather misguided theories to the idea of passive income. One of the most common of them is that you need money to start generating passive income. While some ideas may require an initial startup fee, many require little to no money; merely your initiative to work at it and be consistent.

The other theory I find bandied about is that you need to have a great business idea in order to start making extra income. Venturing into passive income does not require you to become an entrepreneur, but instead rely on tried and trusted ideas that have been used over and over again to build wealth. Some can be as boring as opening up a retirement or savings account that generates extra money over time. Boring, but certainly effective.

Once you do get started, it should be noted that this is NOT an overnight process. You're not suddenly going to create a website or investment in stocks and see returns the next day. Although it was mentioned earlier that they require little to no upkeep, the process of starting up will require you to be consistent and dedicated in your approach to growing your income. Take the time to learn what about the industries you decide to involve yourself in, so that you may be prepared for any trials and challenges that lay ahead. Nothing in life is achieved without some degree of effort, and this is no different.

Within this book, you will find a few different ways to look into developing your passive income, the ins and outs of each type of income and how you could possibly go about getting started. From here, you will be able to achieve a rough guideline into what choices would be available and suitable to your situation, skills and even lifestyle.

Let's dive right in!

Chapter 1: The Right Mind for Your Business

Starting up a business is by no means an easy feat. With that in mind, before we get started, it's important to ensure that you have an idea of what and why it is you would like to start a business. First off, you need to enter the field with the right mindset. Arguably, the mindset is one of the most vital aspects in starting your business, and taking on the challenges that follow in time. So, within this chapter, we will look at the various aspects of being a business owner, and what you need to get started on the right track. In many ways, developing and maintaining a passive income is a form of business. You are creating an avenue for yourself to make money, relying solely on your planning, logic and self-discipline in order to continually build up your income.

One of the important traits to have when getting started, is patience. Planning your own business with the expectation of an immediate return, is unrealistic and will leave you feeling shattered and disappointed. You must be prepared to understand that the goal is longevity, and not immediate wealth. If you were looking for ways to create immediate wealth, I would suggest playing the lottery, or heading to the tables or slot machines at your nearest casinos. What are the chances of your success there? Minimal, if not at all. Playing the long game ensures that you are building a steady and reliable source of income, that will benefit you over the long term, while minimizing risk and, if done the right way, maximizing your rewards (The Human Factor, 2019).

A key mistake, that goes hand in hand with this, is that people will look at a field they have no interest in, because they think it will make them rich. Choosing a field that leaves you feeling satisfied provides a sense of accomplishment and gives you an enjoyment in what it is you are doing. If you find yourself having no pleasure out of the activity, you will probably not pay as much attention to it, as you would had it been something that you did enjoy, and in the end, you will most likely set it aside for something better. When getting started, ask yourself if it is something if the idea you have chosen is something you are passionate about; something that you would enjoy doing. If you find it is not, move on to something that you would. If you didn't like an idea, then it probably wasn't for you. Don't see it as a loss of an option, but instead as an opportunity for something better.

That last statement is critical in developing your business. Remaining positive, and seeing a silver lining in all aspects of the business that you may encounter is powerful. Over the course of your venture into passive income, you may find yourself facing several different challenges that will threaten to bring you down. As an example, maybe you've taken a heavy loss or you've not been able to successfully attract the market to your business for a long time. These would probably be enough to bring anybody down. However, you have to find yourself rising above the idea of falling into despair, or giving up entirely. Failure in business, is most likely going to be an inevitability.

Listen to any successful CEO tell his or her story, and somewhere along the line you will hear about a moment where he or she made mistakes and hit a few stumbling blocks. Treat every moment in failure as a learning venture, and a chance to address your business, so that the same cannot occur again. In this case, you've done something to improve the business and ensure its chances of success. Everything is an opportunity to be better, and this is entirely how you should look at the concept of business. Failure is when we quit. Mistakes are when we learn.

Another mistake one can inevitably make, is not having a plan. If you find yourself heading into a business idea without a plan, a goal, or even an idea of why you started attempting to create a passive income in the first place, you're not going to go very far. A plan then, in this case, is not knowing every step that you are going to take, how much money you will make in five years or how successful your business will be in ten years. Those are merely expectations, and should your business not reach those heights, you will feel naturally disappointed.

A plan starts with the necessary and extensive research into your chosen industry, determining your target market and how you will plan to engage with that market. This would also include planning your finances and cost for anything you may need. Essentially, what you are doing is setting up a plan on how your business is going to start. From there, you can set goals, but they should be based on yourself, not on the market or your expectations of success. For example, if you would like to become a YouTuber, you can start by setting yourself a goal of doing one video every week, or more or less, depending on your own schedule. This way, we can ensure that our goals are being met in from the beginning, and we can feel a sense of accomplishment from what we are doing.

However, this should not stop one from thinking ahead. As a business owner, you need to always be one step ahead. Now, I did not say five or six steps ahead earlier, as mentioned before, because the future is unpredictable. Just a single step. This step is enough to help you to assess the market for your business and adjust accordingly. Take action when it's necessary, not when you feel ready, and don't let outside factors influence the decisions that you will make.

When we are getting started in business, impulsiveness should be one of the furthest things from our way of thinking. Everything will require strategic planning and an understanding of the business as a whole. From there, you can see your business realistically and move forward with this in mind.

Take Responsibility

So far, we have looked at how positivity and a learning mentality is vital in moving your business forward. The mind is arguably one of the most important aspects in creating a business, and will often decide how far you can take it. You can start by insuring that you believe in both yourself, and the business that you are trying to build. This allows you to dedicate yourself fully to the plan you have in mind. As for believing in yourself, having a business idea that plays to your strengths rather than your weaknesses gives you a firm grasp on the tasks on hand. A business that incorporates several of your weaknesses can become a chore and will make you feel listless and frustrated. These are not feelings we want to associate in the business we are developing.

Alongside this, as you are the one solely in charge; you need to be the one to hold yourself accountable. Take responsibility for the paths that you take, and know that the buck stops with you. Nothing is out of your control, and whenever a decision needs to be made, you need to be the one to take action. After all, this is your business. If you do not nurture it, who else is going to do so? Failing to hold yourself accountable, will result in a failure to learn, and a failure to learn will result in a negative pattern that you build for yourself, moving in a cycle around the same mistakes.

So, remember - positivity, determination, acceptance of the idea of failure and accountability are what makes for a successful business venture.

Looking Ahead

Throughout your life, you will encounter people discussing this 'fantastic' business idea they have, or how they've begun to create and develop their own business. Most of the time, the idea is never acted upon, or the business that was being created fades into oblivion, never to be mentioned again. Usually, due to a culmination of the above or a fear to take the plunge into a world they don't quite understand. Starting something on your own takes a lot of guts, and from time to time, you must be willing to take calculated risks. Notice that I say **calculated** risk. If you find yourself taking risks without assessing them properly, you're just playing the lottery all over again. Taking care to ensure that the outcome of the risk is tolerable for both you and your business' needs.

Throughout your business venture, you will need all the skills we have looked at in continuing to ensure that your venture is a worthwhile success. From the startup to an ever-changing and overly dynamic market, to economic 'drama' and unplanned setbacks. You will face a multitude of unforeseen challenges. The key is how you learn, adapt and move past these boundaries in the best manner possible for you. From there, you build the roads that will take you further.

From here, we will move into several unique and creative ways of developing a passive income that you can potentially use to start your journey. Remember to consider your own strengths and weaknesses to judge what would be most applicable to you, as well as your financial status and the interest you have in said field. Look at what you are passionate about and how they will associate with the passive incomes that we will head through. I now leave it all up to you to make the right choice for yourself.

Chapter 2: Dropshipping

Dropshipping is the business model whereby a retail inventory, store or traditional retail arrangement is not required. Instead, the retail company sells the product available, and the order is then transferred to a third-party; a supplier who then delivers the product to the customer. In other words, you sell products that you don't have to stock, ship or even touch. Your drop-shipping supplier does that for you.

Over time, like many of the examples in this book, dropshipping has seen a significant rise in popularity, as it looks to streamline the process in which products are sold and delivered online (Shopify, 2019). In 2017, dropshipping saw a growing market emerge, with approximately 23% percent of all online sales completed via dropshipping, and as time wears on, with the eCommerce market expanding rapidly, it will continue to grow in new and exciting ways.

Irwin Dominguez, is one of the many who saw this emerging market, and looked to take advantage of it, going from zero to **millions** in sales in less than twelve months! An online marketing consultant, Irwin decided to test out the industry after hearing of its success from a friend. After some research, he opened a Shopify account, created a store before adding a few products with Oberlo. With a little marketing and advertising, his business, with little to no capital, blew up in months, and now generates on average around $10,000 per day! (Crazylister.com, 2019)

Another story I am particularly fond of is that of a woman named Kate. It isn't any kind of rags-to-riches story, or a story about neverending struggles on her way to success.

There is nothing really extraordinary about it. That is, in fact, what I like about it.

What is great about this story, is that Kate took something that she had her own personal interest in; in this case, anime (Japanese comics). She took something that she was passionate about, and turned it into something valuable for herself. In this case, netting $32,000 in monthly revenue.

All sounds great, doesn't it? Some entrepreneur makes several thousands of dollars per day not long after starting his business and it's happily ever after? Not quite. I do not want you to go into this process believing that this is a get rich quick scheme. Dropshipping takes a lot of dedication, hard work and planning to be successful, and no two company success stories are the same. Whereas Irwin built his fortune in a few months, some take years and years to really build a customer base to which they can sell these products. Each market is different, and going in expecting instant rewards will disappoint. Change your mindset. Go into the field with the goal of learning, instead of making money, and see and plan out your rise to success from there.

So now that you've heard a little about what dropshipping is, and a few stories of success, let's look at why dropshipping is an attractive industry to move into. Aside from the growing eCommerce market, dropshipping provides you with more flexibility and freedom. You don't have to own a large warehouse, or store products for sales. You don't even need to be in the same country! The business model is fairly easy to grasp, and the startup costs are minimal. With all this, you are offered financial and personal flexibility with which to plan your life between business and pleasure. There are also plenty of helpful tools that you can use to help you when getting started in the dropshipping industry, which is what we will look at now.

Starting Your Own Dropshipping Business.

So you've decided that dropshipping is the option for you, and that this will place you on the journey to reliable passive income. Well, I'm here to help! Throughout this, remember that you are building a brand that represents you. And just like personal growth, we want this brand to reach as high as it possibly can.

Choosing A Niche

The first thing you're going to do is think of the market that you would like to attract. While it's possible to sell just about anything and everything through your store, this will create a cluster of confusion as to what it is that you are offering, and you will struggle to attract a target market. Developing a niche for your business will give you the ability to reach a certain market with your products, and help you build up a client base. So, brainstorm a few ideas. Use your interests, and your hobbies to guide you here. Remember that we're more likely to be successful if it is something we are passionate about. Research more about your chosen field. Find out what people are interested in and where. Look at social media outlets such as Facebook, Instagram, etc. Are there groups that you could use to engage with others as well as share the products that you would like to sell? Of course! You just have to find them!

Once you have decided on a niche, and that there is an established market for it, it is now time to find a supplier for your products. Again, a search engine is your friend here. There are a great deal of online suppliers available, each with their own pros and cons. Dig deep into their websites to determine if the products they offer are suitable for the demands of those you are looking to sell to. As soon as you find the supplier you feel is the best fit, get in touch with them, and find out if they dropship their products, as well as what their requirements are, so that you can negotiate the best deal possible for yourself.

Deciding On A Brand

Now it's time for you to establish your brand. This will define your business, and will guide you into the decisions you will make for your store in the future. Think of all the most popular brands. Think of those that you favor when you purchase something. They invoke a feeling within you. That's how that brand has positioned itself to make you feel.Your brand will be what sets you apart from the others, and why customers will come to you instead.

You'll need a name to start. We don't want to overcomplicate here. Again, think of the best brands. It's simple, short and precise, sliding off the tongue. Try to consider a brand name that is short and easy to say, but will set you apart from the rest.

To go with your brand name, you'll need a slogan. A tagline, in other words. Again, aim to keep it short but catchy.

The final piece of presentation of your brand, is the logo. This will merge with the name and slogan, to create a graphic and hopefully memorable representation of your brand.

Seems like a lot to take in, doesn't it? In reality, this is a simple process that just requires a little creativity. Only one thing left to do for now, and that is to develop a brand story. If you've ever visited a brand website, you'll have noticed an 'About Us' page. This is where you detail into a company's brand story. A brand story is there to inspire an emotional feeling in its audience. Brand stories give your clients something they feel they can associate with, and a reason to stand by your business over others.

Your brand story should define the purpose of your business, and will encompass your merchandise, social media platforms and advertisements. If clients can identify with your brand story, they will buy from you.

Congratulations! You have now created your very own brand!

The Marketplace

Now that you have a supplier and established your very own brand, it is time to set up your online store. There are several eCommerce platforms that will help you along through this, however I would suggest that you use Shopify to set up your store. Shopify offers you a 14-day free trial before commencing with a paid option. The store is very user-friendly and does not require you to have any sort of web development skills in order to create your store.

Within the parameters provided, you can use a variety of tools to make your store suitable to your brand as well aesthetically pleasing to any who may come across it. Don't overthink this, as you'll end up obsessing over it. You can make alterations and improvements to your store over time. The goal for now is to make your store look appealing and interesting to your customers, while allowing it to emphasize the products that you are selling.

Now that you've created your store, it's time to determine what products you will sell. I mentioned niche markets earlier. Keep that in mind now, and structure the products you are selling according to your niche. Make sure to categorize your website, so that clients are able to easily find what they are looking for. Alongside your products, you will have to determine the prices that they will sell for. You will eventually need to fork out a little cash when advertising your products, so keep this in mind when you are determining a price for your products. Try to aim for at least 30% gross profit on each item, if possible.

The final step here is to create your product page. This is the page of your store where clients can view the selected products and it's details. Try to create your own descriptions that entice the customer to buy the product. Remember that in some ways, your store is your salesman.

Once that is done, you've just about completed building your own dropshipping business. Remember that our website should have an 'About Us' page, an 'FAQ Page,' as well as 'Contact Us, Shipping, Refunds and Returns' pages and finally a "Privacy Policy and TOC's" page.

Now you have chosen your niche, established a brand, found your products and created a store. What do we do next? Well, launch, of course! Give yourself a pat on the back. You now run your very own business!

Advertising

The journey we have is far from over. You have a store, but how will people be able to find it? It is time for you to start promoting your store. For starters, you can use your own social media to let others know that you have launched. In turn, you should have already created numerous social media accounts for your business, so that clients have an easy path to finding it as well as communication.

Facebook is the most popular social network in the world, so it makes sense to use them to market your product. Facebook Ads can be a great way to market your products to a select group according to the criteria you determine, such as age, gender, location, etc. This is the first form of advertising you should start with. From there, you may advertise how you see fit.

Don't forget that ads or any other form of marketing is how you will bring clients to your store, so it needs to be appealing and persuasive. It is arguable the biggest aspect of building your client base.

Where To From Here?

Your business is now operating. You have a steady flow of income. So everything is done and dusted, right? You can just sit back and relax? Well, not quite. That is a mistake that I imagine many make. Industries and markets and forever changing. It is your job to monitor these changes and move with them. If your products are no longer selling, it's time to look at alternatives that you think will sell. This can be avoided if you always keep your store up to date according to the latest trends. Make sure that you interact with your customer base. Give them an opportunity to leave reviews of both products *and* services, and engage with them if they are not happy about something.

Don't be an apathetic businessman, otherwise you will find yourself losing business. Remember to be consistent in improvement. If you do not try to improve, your store will stagnate, and that will hinder its growth. Be ambitious. If you constantly strive to improve, you will find yourself reaching higher peaks and taking your business further.

Maybe you will become the next success story that we will read about!

Chapter 3: Amazon FBA

Amazon is widely considered to be the world's largest eCommerce company, according to revenue. They have invested themselves into several aspects of eCommerce, with one of those aspects being Amazon FBA.

Fulfillment by Amazon (FBA) is a service that provides storage, packaging and shipping assistance to sellers. Unlike dropshipping, where you do not own any merchandise, Amazon FBA has you invest in merchandise that is then stored at one of their warehouses. The products are packed and shipped, all courtesy of Amazon.

This works to your benefit, as you have the credibility of Amazon being associated with your products, and customers will feel they are more likely to receive quality products through your business. On top of this, you will never have to handle any merchandise, which can take the burden off of handling and maneuvering large volumes of equipment. Using Amazon FBA also means that you will pay lower shipping fees, due to their relationships with certain shipping companies.

As I am sure you have already guessed, using Amazon's services will cost you a bit of money. Amazon will take approximately 15% of your product price once it is sold, along with storage, shipping and handling fees that you will have to pay.

Now you may be thinking that dropshipping is already a better alternative, as you avoid having to pay several fees, however each comes with its own perks according to your business model.

With dropshipping, you are required to build up a client base in order to sell your product. However, Amazon allows you to bypass some of this, as you have access to their huge customer base, while increasing your profit margins due to a higher selling price, courtesy, again, of the Amazon brand.

Naturally, you will have doubts about involving any of the giant-size brands in your startup business, such as Amazon, there is much success to be made from this kind of business model. Amazon FBA's profit margins and branching revenue streams make it possible to greatly increase the earning potential for your business.

Spencer Haws, owner of Niche Pursuits, used this to his advantage, selling his products on Amazon and raking in approximately $40,000 dollars in his first month. This just shows that there is tremendous potential for profits within the industry, just in merely finding the right niche. The possibilities that await are potentially endless!

Building Your Amazon FBA Business

So now that you're interested in starting your own Amazon FBA business, where do you actually begin?

Open an account and consider your niche

Well, the first step is to open a 'Seller Account' with Amazon. You can either opt for a Professional or an Individual account. The Individual account does not require any monthly subscription, however you will have several limitations placed on your account. These could work for you, or against you, depending on the needs of your business.

Just as you would do in dropshipping, you will need to find a niche for your business. Remember to relate it to something that you're interested in, such as a hobby or special interest. Don't throw away extra ideas you may have, as you could potentially add them in the future, or use them as an alternative if your current niche is not turning out successfully. As always, expand your knowledge as much as possible, so that you can better determine the best possible outcomes for your business.

What products will you sell?

From there, you will need to determine what products you would like to sell. Consider using keyword tools to help you gather research into how often people search for certain products, and use this to determine what are the best products to sell.

Make sure to identify what fees are associated with each product. Weight, size and storage requirements will vary depending on your product, so look for products with lower fees to minimize your expenses.

Do your best to keep away from products that are used by popular brand names and are well-established in the markets. These are infinitely harder to compete with.

Product Sourcing

Once you've determined the core products that your niche will center around, you will need to find out where your products will be sourced from. You should be looking for supplies with high quality products available for you to sell.

If you intend to sell a product that is produced locally, you could head to your local manufacturer and I'm positive they will be welcoming to your efforts.Alternatively, you could still take the route of using an overseas supplier, which is also beneficial as it tends to bring potential for higher profit margins for your business.It would be to your own benefit to test the products that you are planning on selling, should you find yourself sourcing from an overseas supplier. Try to get your hands on some samples so that you can ensure you will be providing high quality items to your future clients.

Your next step will be to ship the goods to an Amazon Fulfillment Center. Amazon will provide you with specifications and instructions when going through this process. Be sure to keep shipping costs in mind, as these can derail your business if you fail to keep track of them.

Creating your brand

You now have products ready to be sold, however, you're still going to need a brand. Your brand will tell your clients who you are. Make sure to research if your brand name has already been used or not, as well as whether there is an available domain. Your domain name is your website's name, and this will be where clients are able to find you.

Even though you gain more brand will gain more credibility through Amazon, it is still important for you to place high value on its creation. This will define your business for as long as it exists, and so you need to make sure it starts off on the right foot. Remember the main facets of a brand are its name, tagline, logo and the brand story. This will also include your products and how you choose to display them.

Create your product pages, making sure your product details are accurate and detailed, while product photos are professional that emphasize and show off your products. Take a look around to see how other brands market their own products, using this to guide you in your own marketing.

Make sure the tone of your descriptions are friendly and enticing to potential buyers. 'Sell' the product, but don't let them feel that you are selling it. Use the descriptions to make clients feel like this is something they **must** buy; that they can't live without. Be expressive in your writing. Make sure any paragraphs you have are structured and organized so that they are attractive to the reader. Too much boxed all together will feel a little overwhelming.

The aim of the description is to sell the product, and to silence all doubts a client may have regarding their purchase.

Marketing

Your Amazon FBA business is all set up. Now we have to market it. As it is with dropshipping, advertising is the key component to get your business up and running and bring in sales.

Social media is still your best friend here. Look at enhancing your brand's profile, allowing people to view, like, comment and share as you go along. This ensures that you begin to build a rapport with potential customers.

However, don't rush yourself into exploring several channels for marketing at once, and try to invest time in all of them simultaneously. Instead, select a few channels or platforms to begin with, and once you feel you are gaining a return, you can move onto something else.

Here, there is a benefit to influencers, as you can use them to market your product for you. Offer them free products in return for reviewing and marketing your products, and you may see your sales gain a significant boost.

On top of this, consider adding platforms on your website and social media for clients to leave reviews of their purchases and service, as great reviews can give you a massive reputation boost for future customers. Drive your current and potential customers to sign up for email subscriptions. Use your website to find interesting, but not overwhelming ways of enticing your clients to sign up for a subscription. (Smale, 2019)

A Few Extra Tips

Make it a consistent goal to improve your Best Sellers Rank (BSR). The term being fairly self-explanatory, having a business with consistent BSR growth will show clients that your business has tremendous potential to succeed, and that you are reliable in the quality that you offer.

Stay ahead of the trends, and provide more offers to your clients whenever possible. Continue to include products that will compliment the ones that you already have yet provide more variety in selection.

You could also continue to increase your revenues by becoming an affiliate with

Amazon. However, we'll discuss affiliate marketing in detail a little later.

With Amazon's extensive brand and tools available to you, there is a world of endless possibilities that await you, should you choose Amazon FBA to further your venture.

Chapter 4: Affiliate Marketing

Now, as previously mentioned, we'll move onto affiliate marketing. If you've heard of affiliate marketing before, I imagine you're thinking it may be complicated and not worth the effort. However, if you've done any prior research on passive income previously, you'd know that affiliate marketing is considered one of the go-to opportunities when it comes to passive income.

So what is affiliate marketing?

Affiliate marketing is the process with which you can earn commission by promoting another company or person's products. Although revenue is earned through different pay schemes, the general idea is that you will earn an income for each sale you make on the product that you have successfully marketed. This adds legitimacy to the term "Get Paid as you Sleep," as you will earn revenue every time someone uses your affiliate code, or clicks on the link that you have provided. The potential income you receive can vary wildly, from a few bucks here to thousands and possibly even millions. It is all about the manner in which you promote, the traffic you receive, and how you use the skills you have acquired to persuade your clients to purchase something.

Unlike dropshipping and Amazon FBA, you are not in any directly involved with the products, their purchasing or their shipping. You are solely responsible for the marketing of that product. However, this does not mean you should become an affiliate for just about anything. You are not just representing a product, as the product is also representing you and your credibility with clients. The emphasis here is still to ensure that you are associated with high quality products that will help in establishing trust and reliability with your clients.

Even if you've never traveled, I am sure that you've heard of TripAdvisor before. TripAdvisor is a website designed to provide helpful hints, tips and suggestions on places such as hotels and restaurants in various locations around the globe. And guess what? TripAdvisor is an affiliate! You would never have even guessed it, yet the site receives around 116 million visitors every month, earning income from travel companies, hotels as well as other travel sites. They are perhaps one of the largest success stories of affiliate marketing.

Again, not everyone is guaranteed this side of success. However, it could help to merely supplement your salary and ensure that you will live comfortably, or buy that car that you've always wanted. Remember that we are not trying to engage in get rich quick schemes. We are aiming to create an environment where we can live our lives with purpose, while pursuing our dreams. At the end of the tunnel, the reward is very much worth the risk, if you have played the right cards.

Creating an Affiliate Marketing Scheme

As with all of the forms of passive income we have looked at so far, you will need to find a niche for which you can become an affiliate. You might be asking, "If it's just advertising, why do I have to find a niche?" Well, for one, it provides your website with a more organization and structure, and allows you to attract a market, rather than going for the general public. When people are searching for a certain product or service, you will want them to be attracted to your website, and from there to go on and purchase something. This is the advantage of a niche market. Remember the example of TripAdvisor? They provide various options and suggestions for aspiring travelers to consider when planning their holiday. That is their niche.

In this case, it is wise to also consider whether there is space for another affiliate marketer within your chosen niche. Just like you would tend to avoid entering a product market that competes with the largest brands, it is preferable to avoid entering a bloated affiliate market. Are you able to provide competition and make a return? If the answer is yes, then by all means, go for it! Consider a niche that has a broad space for affiliates, so that your options for revenue remain as expansive as possible.

Research is key

From there, it is time to start researching affiliate programs, in order to decipher the products that you will aim to promote. Don't be afraid of taking your time in making the right choice, as it will be well worth your while in the end!

Look for programs that have higher returns and are more profitable. Keep in mind that physical products usually generate lower commission rates than informative products and services. However, each one of these can most certainly be just as profitable as the other. You have to consider what is right for you.

As an example, if you find yourself promoting physical products, signing up with Amazon's affiliate program gives you a 24-hour commission bonus. What this means, is that any product sold in the 24 hours after a customer clicks your link will grant you the commission. Others have long programs, from a month to 90 days. It's up to you to determine the right fit.

Create your website

Now it's time for you to build a site. To begin, you will have to purchase a domain. The domain is the address of your website. NameCheap and DreamHost are two options to consider, however there are several more that are available. Look for an option to purchase that meets your financial constraints.

Once you have done that, it is now time to purchase and setup a host. The host is the place where you will find your site. It is where the entirety of your site resides. Both hosting and domain purchases are fairly affordable, so don't be afraid to move forward, as it neither will be too costly, provided you find the right option for you. Although you will have to take into consideration your financial ability, avoid going for the cheapest option for web hosts. Look for reliable, quality hosting platforms such as BlueHost or HostGator.

Once you've established a host, you're going to need a Content Management System. CMS, for short. CMS is software provided to you, allowing you to create and manage a website without any need for technical, in-depth knowledge of web development or design. This streamlines the process of creating a website, as you don't have to learn any sort of programming in order to start building your website.

If you're a beginner to building a website using CMS, consider using WordPress as it is user friendly and fairly straightforward. However, the choice is yours if you'd prefer another platform. Try to keep it simple in your creation, as you might find yourself overcomplicating things if you're trying to add too much visual appeal. A simple theme will do.

Website Content

The next step is to create content for your site. Your content should remain relevant to your niche, while remaining intriguing and engaging with your target audience. Your content should be interesting enough to retain your existing audience, while still bringing in new members. Product reviews can be useful to provide your clients with assistance in determining what are the best products for them to consider. You could be providing comparison quotes, as a way of seeing how one product matches up against the other. Think of times when you were unsure what smartphone to purchase. You probably looked online to compare the devices to see which would be the best for you.

Another alternative is blog posting. Blogs ensure that you have a consistent structure to building content on your site. Alongside all of this, consider dishing out free informational products, such as an email subscription series, or an ebook. This can help to generate more interest in any product you are trying to sell.

Building a follower base

Once this is complete, it is now time for you to build your audience. If your content is of the highest level, you will eventually start bringing traffic through to your site consistently.

Here, follow the same methods that you would always use. Turn to social media. Another potential option is to use someone else's audience to build your own. Consider writing content for a few blogs whose traffic is fairly high. Remember to make sure that these blogs are also relevant to your niche. You will garner less attraction if you decide to engage with a completely different market, and that is not healthy for your prospects.

If you have the financial capability, you may want to consider investing in paid advertising.

Advertising in the right places can definitely improve the traffic to your site. You may also consider the prospect of SEO. Search Engine Optimization(SEO) is the process of attempting to boost your search engine ranking. What does this mean? Well, if you find yourself looking for a website to purchase video games online, you will naturally use a search engine. When you do, I am positive that you do not sift through the hundreds of pages that are dished out to you. Instead you probably look at the links found on the first page. The aim of SEO is to be on that first page. Think about that for a second. Imagine that when people are searching for something related to your niche, your website is the first to show up. This could potentially drive your traffic through the roof!

Consider hiring an SEO professional, or taking the time to learn it yourself, using their techniques and principles in order to build your audience. (Ogle, 2019)

Promoting Your Offers

Now that you have built up an audience, it is time to kickstart your promotions! You have already shown people that the content you provide is interesting and relevant to them. Now they are willing to listen to you. Promoting content can be done in a variety of ways, depending on you and your site.

One of these techniques is "In-text links." While your audience is reading your content, they may come across links to certain products or services. Should they decide to click on the link and purchase that product or service, you will make a commission on the sale. In-text links are a subtle but effective way of promoting offers, as they are structured around your content, and ensure that your audience is not being bombarded with a sales pitch, which they may not appreciate.

Another option, mentioned previously, are product reviews. Once your audience is willing to listen to and trust you, they will be more accepting and reliant on your opinion. The idea here is not just to point out all of the positives and ignore the negatives. You will need to be honest about your own experience of the product and your thoughts of it in general. It would be better appreciated if you are specific, and describe your offer and product in great detail. From there, you can provide your affiliate link to the offer, and should it be purchased, you've made a sale!

Affiliate Marketing is mostly about quality and strategy. The strategy you have, to develop quality content, and from there, market your affiliate products. You'll notice that the very last thing mentioned was making a sale. That's because we started with the planning and development, and from there looked to develop the quality needed to attract people. Then it was about promoting our affiliate products effectively. Once that happened, it would now be possible to make a sale. You will find that most of these steps will be repeated consistently throughout your venture as an affiliate marketer. However, the sale should be the furthest thing from your mind. Let it happen naturally, rather than trying to force a sale.

If you follow the steps, and you have researched the markets in-depth, I have no doubt that great success can be achieved on your road to true prosperity.

Chapter 5: Blogging

Unlike many of other passive income sources listed in this book, blogging is one of those that most people have been well aware of, but never quite learned too much about it.

What is a Blog?

Simply put, a blog is a sort of online diary. These blogs can be used for the individual, or engaging with others as a more public use. These blogs can include pictures, videos or just plain old-fashioned text.

Started in 1994, blogs have gone from strength to strength in a variety of different categories; from networking, to collective hobby interests to advertising and promotion. Unlike many other aspects of the Internet, instead of being upstaged by other platforms, blogging has diversified its uses. Out of approximately 2 billion websites that exist on the Internet, hundreds of millions of them are blogs. One blogging platform can have around 400 million blogs and users alone, showing their incredible growth and popularity.

As a blogger, you will have the freedom of being able to work whenever and wherever you want, while making money from it. In essence, blogging is the passion, and money can be an added benefit. Blogging gives us the ability to do what we love, while earning money for it. That's what we want, right? Of course!

However, how can this be used to earn any income? Well, that is entirely dependent on you. As mentioned earlier, including affiliate offers within your blogs can help you to earn an income while performing a hobby and sharing your interest.

An alternative to this, would be to sell advertising on your site. This will usually require you to have a very large stream of traffic to have any sort of meaningful return. Usually, I would suggest that this act as a supplement to another source of passive income.

Generally, with blogging, the idea will be to combine with other forms of passive income to create the revenue. A first example would be dropshipping. You could offer products relevant to your blog for others to consider for purchase. So if you have a blog centered around makeup, you could offer cosmetics for others to use as a way of generating income.

Two other alternatives, which we'll discuss in greater detail later in this book, are selling e-books or online courses. This may mean that your initial involvement may be substantially increased, but the rewards for it are increasingly justified, especially since there are zero costs involved in the creation of these products.

The ideas you use will depend on the type of blog you want to create, and the skills you possess that will benefit your business.

Your Own Blog Site

So you've decided to start your own blog. Well, I'm going to sound like a stuck record at this point, but again, you have to start by choosing a niche. However, this time, things are a little different. Whereas in previous chapters, you would choose a niche based on your personal interest and its profitability; this time, you would choose a niche solely based on your personal knowledge and interests, where there is generally a common interest.

There are over 8 billion people in the world today. Somehow choosing a niche that nobody is interested in is most certainly going to be a hard task for anyone at this point. If you fancy a blog based on the theory that the world is flat, I am sure that you will find an audience looking to engage in this thoughtful endeavor with you. Likewise, if you want to write up a blog detailing your belief that aliens live on Mars, you could probably find support for that too!

Granted, most of us wouldn't be so outlandish, and so the niche you fill yourself into would generally be one where there is a large collective interest. What matters is how you manage to reach that audience. However, we'll reach that point a little later. To begin, you have to actually create a blog.

What will you need to begin your first blog? A blogging platform, of course. Choosing the right blogging platform is essential to your needs and skills. To start, you need to consider the type of blog you would like to have.

Is it going to be predominantly text-based, or will it be incredibly picture heavy? For example, if you wanted something text-based, you could use WordPress, which is fairly popular and easy to use, however if you needed a platform that would accommodate a blog that is focused around images, then you would consider Tumblr. If you were looking for something that was more of a mixture, then you could consider Medium.

How much experience do you have when it comes to blogging? Can you handle a platform with severely advanced customization, or do you need something a little more beginner friendly?

Does the blogging platform have any restrictions when it comes to monetization. This is integral, as you don't want to start up a blog on one platform, only to realize that your suggested revenue stream is against their policies.

Finally, what are your financial constraints? Some blogging platforms will require you to have a subscription, while others like WordPress are completely free, however you will have to front the cost for the purchase of a domain.

These are all questions that you will need to ask yourself before you decide to move forward, to avoid any potential hiccups along the way.

As always with having your own website, you need to purchase a domain and a web host to allow the site to run online. Once again, find the options that are cost effective for you, while maintaining quality.

Building Your Blog

The next step is to plan the details of your blog.

What is the aim of your blog, and how much time are you willing to donate to blogging? The aim is something you probably already know, given you have determined your niche as well, but on top of that, you need to consider the amount of time that you have. Granted, you may have a full-time job, kids, or many other factors that keep you occupied. Blogging has to work around this, to ensure that you are still organized in your daily life, and won't leave this behind when you feel notably overwhelmed.

What feelings do you want to invoke in your audience? This helps to determine the tone and setting of your blog. It will ensure that you are finding and writing the right material centered around the aim that you wish to create.

And lastly, how will you manage to attract your audience into using any

one of your chosen revenue streams? Look at how you will plan to market these streams, and what steps to take to persuade your audience into a purchase. This should be the last thing to consider, as it will be based around the content you wish to create, and so ensuring quality content should be your foremost priority.

Now you have a plan, and it is time to design your blog on your chosen platform. It's okay to be tempted to go nuts on the creation, however you'd do well to keep it simple to start. As your experience grows, and you have an idea of using design as a focused point of attraction, you can modify however you see fit. For now, it just needs to be neat and well presented. That, in itself, is interesting to a potential audience. A cluttered blog will merely drive them away. Look at it from the perspective of the audience that you aim to attract and move from there.

Once this is done, it's time to get writing! This part is entirely of your own doing.

Promotion is integral

Now that you have a blog up and running with a few posts, it's time to promote your blog. At this point, I'm sure you know the basics of promoting a few forms of passive income. If your blog contains images, consider using Pinterest and Instagram to promote snippets of your blog, so that others will be keen to see more. As we mentioned with affiliate marketing, consider using other more popular blogs to build up and develop your audience. Use email marketing as a way to notify your current readers of upcoming posts, to ensure they continue coming back for more.

Monetization

Now you need to monetize your blog. As I said earlier, there are several ways you can go about this. If your blog has potential for products that are relevant to your niche, consider dropshipping or affiliate marketing.

As your blog continues to grow in popularity, you may begin to receive offers from advertisers, looking for their own opportunities. You could choose to sell them advertising space directly, or an alternative could be to use Google Adsense, streamlining the process and removing the direct content. We'll learn more about Google Adsense in an upcoming chapter.

The benefits of a blog is that you can combine several aspects of passive income together, although I wouldn't suggest doing that, as you don't want your blog to come across as a money making scheme. Bar the case of ad space, your income form should supplement and be relevant to your content and vice versa, so that there is a direct association between the two.

With the right attitude, blogging could be one of the most engaging and pleasurable ventures that you could potentially immerse yourself in.

Chapter 6: Kindle Publishing

If you find that you have a talent for writing, or you already spend time writing as a hobby, then Kindle Direct Publishing (KDP) may be a fantastic option for you. Usually, if you would like to publish a book you've written, there are two ways to go about it. Having it published by a publishing house, which arouses the possibility of being rejected, or self-publishing, where you take on the decision to publish the book yourself. Given Amazon holds onto a vast majority of the eBook market, they would be the logical choice to use in the case of self-publishing.

Amazon Kindle Direct Publishing allows authors to independently publish their own works on the Kindle store platform (Written Word Media, 2019). On top of being the leaders of the eBook world, they have introduced a paperback option, which provides an alternative to those who prefer the look and feel of a book between their fingers.

Usually, in these cases, the traditional market trumps the newer market in all aspects but one: convenience. However, with self-publishing, that is not entirely true. The self-publishing market has several benefits over the traditional market, especially and most importantly in terms of time. The time it takes to secure a publishing deal can vary from months to years. In today's world, that would be insanity, given you could simply sign up on Amazon and have your book published the very same day, and payment arriving in a few months.

Crucially, the self-publishing market allows you to reach the entire global market, freeing you up for even greater potential for income along the way. Kindle is a fantastic platform for indie authors to finally get their works out there, and start earning an income on them. In terms of royalties, Amazon offers about 60% more than the average publishing house, ensuring your earning potential is much greater if you manage to achieve a decent amount of sales. This really is a fantastic market for anyone who sees writing as a hobby, as the work involved aside from the writing is minimal, and allows you to focus your passion into a reliable income.

Where to Begin

Although you may be inclined to think that once you have written your book, you can pass it off for Amazon, and that will be that; that is not the case. There are several things you need to consider once your book is complete.

Designing your book

So let's look at the following scenario...You have a book. You have the title, the words, the description. What now? Well, consider all the eBooks you've come across, as well as the books you have and see in stores everywhere.

Let's begin with the title. Your title should build up a sense of curiosity in a potential reader's mind. It should intrigue and capture them; make them want to know more. Here is where your cover design complements your title. You need a cover design that is bold and interesting, while complementing your title. We've all seen that some of the best books have the most amazing cover designs. The fact of the matter is, there really isn't much option of reading the first 100 pages to determine whether this is something interesting, so you have to capture their visual senses with the design, and their emotional senses with the title.

A word of warning to the wise. Unless you've professionally designed a cover before, don't do it. This is where quality needs to be at its highest, and you may need to be prepared to spend a bit of money to make more money. There are plenty of publishing companies and individuals that would be happy to help here, for a price. If you're on a really tight budget, you could consider Fiverr, however make sure the designer's samples are of a reasonable quality.

The next step to consider is what the inside of your book looks like. Is it written in a font that is pleasing on the eye? Is it structured and organized and easy to read? You could have answered yes to all of these questions, but I would still suggest that you take the time to hire a professional editor or editing software. With the editing software, you can paste in your content and it will change the formatting before passing it back to you. I personally prefer the human option, as an editor can benefit you in using formatting that can be emotive and correspondent with your writing tone and style. Something an artificial intelligence is not capable of. Once this is done, be sure to proofread it using Kindle, to ensure there aren't any further issues that need to be fixed.

Now, I would be remiss if I failed to mention book description. It is a common misconception that the entire purpose of the description is merely to provide a summary of what the book is about. It is irrelevant whether the book is fiction or nonfiction. The purpose of your description, along with your title and cover design, is to make the reader believe they **need** to read your book. They need to believe it is a necessity before they can continue on with their lives.

In the case of nonfiction, the description should include a little detail on the purpose of the book, the benefit to reading the book, using emotive adjectives to convey emotions into the reader, as well as a call to action. A call to action gives the suggestion to readers that they should buy your book. Sounds rather basic, but altogether this actually works.

In the case of fiction, you'd want to create a scenario for your reader. Remember that you're trying to be mysterious about the contents of your book. By the end of your description, the reader should have more questions than answers. Don't make the mistake of mixing curiosity with confusion. Your book description should still be understandable and intriguing, but must have the reader desperately wanting to know what happens next. That desperation could lead them to buy your book.

You could say that all of this is the first step in the marketing of your book. It's your presentation, so to speak.

Publishing

Now that you have your book, it's time to have it published. However, you have two options to consider. The first is Kindle Direct Publishing. The second is KDP Select. Both of these options are the same in almost all regards except one. KDP Select requires you to be entirely exclusive. What this means is that your eBook cannot be sold anywhere else. Given that we know that Amazon controls most of the eBook market, this isn't too much of a loss. However, it's up to you and what options you would like to have available to you.

Make sure you can place your book in the correct categories, so that if someone is searching related to your book, they could potentially stumble on your book. Look for other books within the category that match up with some of the aspects of your book.

From there, determine your price for it, and publish! Really? It's not that simple? Yes, it is! Publish the book!

Moving Even Further

If this is your first book, chances are you're going to get off to a slow start. Once the first book is published, I would suggest that you begin to put preparations in place to promote any potential titles in the future.

One of the features you can introduce is a review system. Consider starting up a blog or providing a social media link, where they can leave their reviews based on the book they've read. Encourage readers to leave their honest opinions, providing something to make it worth their while, such as a discount on your next book or a free printed version. You can also use your blog or social media account to inform your readers of any future projects you have in mind and once they have been completed. Consider finding out what your readers like to read about. Chances are that these will be closely related to what you have written, anyway.

Once you are ready to publish your next book, consider handing out a few free copies of the book to your readers before release, so that they have time to review it beforehand. This will give your book more credibility once it hits the virtual shelf', and can aid in bringing more customers to your works. Send out emails to your loyal readers a week before launch, so that they are ready to purchase it upon release.

If you'd like to focus a bit on the monetary side of things, then I would consider shifting your price up once a week after release. Usually this is because you would release your book at a lower rate than usual, but raise it from there. Notify your readers that you will be changing the price, as this gives them an incentive to rush to buy the book. Nobody likes missing out on a great deal!

Although these are some of the things you can do to help in boosting your potential sales, the main aspect of this passive income is always going to be your book. If your book resonates with its readers and proves a legitimate success, you're more likely to retain those readers and they may even pass on recommendations to their friends and family. As more people read your book, more people will be interested in your work, and more people will recommend you. This can be quite fulfilling, as you are doing something that you absolutely enjoy, and others are loving it just as much!

Chapter 7: Social Media Marketing

Ah. Social Media. In the current age, I don't see any of us living without it. Useful in so many ways, from keeping in contact with long-lost family and friends to developing and reaching out to the audience of your business. As you've seen so far, social media will play a big role in any business venture you turn to, as it is the one thing that is most easily accessible to everyone.

So what is social media marketing?

It's fairly self-explanatory. It is the process of using various social media platforms to build and engage with an audience in order to develop your brand or drive traffic to a website. So how can you build a passive income out of this? Well, as mentioned previously, you could use it to drive sales in one of your other forms of income. However, since we are looking at using it as a form of passive income, one thing to consider is starting your own marketing agency.

Like many forms of passive income, a social media marketing agency gives you the freedom of being able to work anywhere, anytime, while giving you a platform into a business with tremendous earning potential. As an agency, you will be there to help other brands grow their business and promote brand loyalty. You will be responsible for engaging with their customers as well as the advertising that is needed. Once you gain reasonable success, you can then begin to take on new clients and take your own brand to greater heights.

How Do I Start My Own Brand?

Stepping into the social media marketing world, is stepping into a vastly expanding industry, so you must be prepared to put in a decent amount of work and stake your claim as a more persuasive choice than other marketers in the field. First, we need to build up your business.

Have a business plan

To begin, you need to develop your business plan. You may need to spend some time investing in yourself, as if you haven't done any kind of social media marketing before, you don't really want to head into this flying blind. Extensive research will be needed. Consider doing a few free courses, as well as few paid ones as well. Once you feel you have gathered as much knowledge as you possibly can about the industry, it is time to step in.

Consider building a portfolio of services that you would like to offer your future customers.

This will provide other brands with clarity on the strategies you will use in the services and solutions that you plan to offer. Will you be able to offer analytics or content marketing, or both? Try to find offers that your clients would not find at other social media agencies, in order to set yourself apart.

Professional Links

Next, businesses will need a way to find you. So, you will need to set up a website. As we've gone through this book, I'm sure you've become aware of the processes involved in building a website. Your website should contain all the details on the services you provide, their prices, and contact information. Consider adding details on why you would be a superior choice to any other agency.

Once your website is complete, you need to set up your own agency's social media accounts. It is vital that you have your own presence on social media, is clients would become a bit skeptical to your expertise, if they find that you are not active in that field. Social media will also be the location that you will use to begin marketing your services. Your posts and content on social media will provide a demonstration of skills that you have learned. Use the tools that various social media providers offer to generate wide reaching engagement and increase the number of people you can potentially reach.

Make sure that you provide links to both your website and your social media accounts from each, so that clients can find all of your information easily.

Something you may want to consider, is to start up a blog on your website. You can use these blogs to further demonstrate your understanding and skills in the field. Creating how-to articles, trend coverage and tips posted on your blog will show others that your knowledge is extensive, and would make them more comfortable with considering you as a suitable hiring choice. As a newcomer in the market, your activity on social media platforms as well as the content on your blog will add some credibility to your agency.

Once you have all the basics in place, you will need to find clients who are willing to work with you. Don't think of the big companies just yet. They will most definitely not consider hiring someone without a proven track record. To begin, you need to approach the smaller companies in the hope that you will pick up a few clients. Cold mailing is one of the strategies you can use to pitch yourself to potential clients. Cold mail is reaching out to someone directly without any form of prior contact. Usually, this is used to describe emails that have been sent, but in this case I would suggest using LinkedIn. LinkedIn is a professional social network, designed to help people make business connections and share their expertise, experience and potential find employment. You can message potential clients here describing the services that you provide and why they should hire you.

Consider adding a promotional aspect into your message. For example, should they hire you, they will pay a reduced fee for a short time period, or alternatively, offer a free trial to build confidence in your service.

Always make sure that you are keeping up with the latest trends in social media marketing. You should be keeping an eye on your rivals to make sure that you are always one step ahead, using the latest features and tools that have been introduced on each platform. Even falling slightly behind in the industry can mean you suffer a big loss as competition until the emergence of the next trend you can jump on.

For your social media marketing agency to be successful, the most important thing you need is results. Results will in turn bring more clients. More clients will in turn bring more revenue. However, your main focus should be the quality that you display. Clients will not be impressed if you fail to deliver the services you offered. Even if you have to start with just a single client, prioritize quality over quantity, and the rest will come with it.

A Few Tips Of Note

Once you've developed your social media marketing agency, picked up a few clients and achieved reasonable success, you're going to want to maintain any potential growth. Leaving your agency to stagnate will mean it will fall behind other companies and lose potential clients as time wades on, so you need to be organized and consistent in your approach.

Once you've picked up a few clients and have been fairly successful with them, consider adding a review aspect to your website, linking them with the reviews in order to boost your credibility for the future.

Be open to changing your strategy from time to time. Sometimes, a single strategy will not work in all given scenarios, and you may need to be more flexible to meet your client's and their customers' needs. Always be prepared to analyze and understand how you can position yourself to deliver exceptional quality in every scenario.

Always research your audience. Making assumptions about what you believe your audience will appreciate can be a dangerous game. Make sure that you use all of the tools available to you to find out as much as possible about your audience demographics on each social network.

Using this knowledge, make engagement a priority. The level of engagement you have determines how your audience perceives you and their willingness to interact. You want your audience to feel like they play an active part of the company in your interaction with them. Make sure to strike the right balance with them. You don't want to add too much personality that it takes from the promotional. However, you don't want to be too promotional as this will drive away some of your audience.

Something you should look at for personal development is to set goals for yourself. Set goals that tackle your largest challenges. It could be to add more personality and be more engaging, or be more persuasive in your advertising. This makes sure you are ever improving and developing your expertise, and will benefit your business in the long run. Remember there is always something new that can be learned. You should never stop learning.

There are probably several more useful tips and tricks. However, I believe if this is your chosen field for passive income, you will come across them during the time you spend learning the skills you need, as well as during your time as a social media marketer.

For now, you have all the necessary steps to build your way into the industry and gain the income you desire. From there, the potential of your business is only limited by how far you are willing to take it.

Will you reach for the sky? Or will you reach for the stars? The choice is yours.

Chapter 8: Rental Income

The housing market is probably one of the most enormous markets in the world. Why? We all need somewhere to stay, or we need a premises to act as the base of our business operations.

Part of this market is the rental market. When most people are unable or unwilling to purchase a property, they may choose to rent instead. While selling a property results in the seller receiving a bulk payment at the value of the property, rentals provide you with a fixed monthly income at a fee you set for your property for a duration of time.

Renting gives you the opportunity to earn enough income to cover the costs of that property that you have to fill, and provide you with extra as well. Of course, there are certain risks involved. You could end up with a destructive tenant, or a non-paying tenant. However, one could say that no form of passive income is without its risks, and this is no different. You will have to do the right amount of research into your potential customers before renting out the property.

While the housing market is fairly straightforward, there are a few things to consider to make sure you can get the most out of your business, with reduced risk. If you have another property where you do not live, or an outbuilding attached to your home that is not in use, then a rental income might be the right way forward for you.

Renting Out Your Property

You need to consider your own property first when planning a rental. What type of property is it? Are your tenants going to be using it for residential purposes or business purposes. You will have to decide if the property is in sufficient shape to be offered out. If not, you may need to invest a little in repairing anything that is damaged or broken, while making it look attractive as possible. Remember, you want to find tenants who will be happy living in your premises. This will mean they are more likely to be reliable and pay their bills on time.

From there, consider your neighbourhood, the features of your property and its condition as well. This will help you in determining the price of your rental. The general rule is that your rental fee is in the area around 1% of your home's entire value. However, it's important to note that some places may have control over your rental rate. New York, Maryland and Washington all have varying degrees of rent control laws, so you need to do some extensive research on the rental market and its jurisdictions in your area.

Individual vs. Agency

Once your property is in decent shape, and you have an idea of how much you are going to rent it for, you can plan on renting out your property.

There are two ways to go about this. You could choose to hire an agency who will take care of the business for you, or you could choose to do it yourself. There isn't too much harm in doing it yourself, provided you actually know what you are doing.

There are benefits to both, and the rental agency offers you the benefit of having a tried-and-tested procedure when it comes to renting out properties to tenants. They will streamline the process for you, and handle all the paperwork and communication from the tenant, relaying it back to you. You generally don't have much, if anything to do with the process. The downside being that agents can charge a hefty fee for their services - generally 10% of the rental amount.

On the other hand, you could research the processes and follow them yourself. However, some tenants may have a belief that it's easier to take advantage of individual home owners instead of those who went through an agency. Should any issues occur, you may find yourself struggling with the procedures to follow. In the case of an agency, they will know the direct route to take, and follow it to the tee.

Warning signs to be aware of

However in this case, let's just assume you want to rent your property out independently. You will need to learn how to vet your potential tenants. This is arguably one of the most important aspects of renting. You need to inspect a prospective tenant's past behavior in the form of a credit profile as well as their tenant profile to determine that they have been consistent, and that there are no red flags to consider. Past behavior is usually an indicator of future behavior, so it's best to avoid all clients who have any hiccups on their profiles.

There are a few suspicious behaviors that you will need to be aware of going in. For example, a tenant who asks to enter an agreement in an alternative family member's name, outside of the person responsible for the property, is a sufficient enough risk to consider moving on and finding an alternative tenant.

Another red flag would be a potential tenant who tries to negotiate on the initial sum to be paid. If a tenant asks to pay the initial fee in parts, this may indicate a lack of affordability and will paint a negative picture of their future actions.

Make sure to evaluate your pet policies. Will pets be allowed into your property? If you do allow pets, what pets are suitable to the type of accommodation you are providing.

Finally, evaluate the type of tenants you would like to have. Younger tenants are more likely to cause harm to your property, as well as tenants that have children. Look for tenants who seem responsible and stable in their lives.

Rental Structure

Once you feel that you have a firm grasp on what to look out for, you need to draw up a leasing agreement in advance. This means you are suitably prepared once you have found a tenant that is up to your standards.

Usually, it's possible to find a lease template online; however, it is up to you to ensure that your lease has all the necessary sections and subsections to satisfy your needs.

As an example, some of the more general aspects of the lease to include are:

Tenant Names. This is not just the name of the person responsible, but all tenants on the property.

Length of Tenancy. All rental documents should state how long the term of the lease runs for. You could either have a rental agreement, which runs from month to month and self-renews until terminated, or a fixed-term lease, which usually lasts about a year.

Rental Fee. This should specify the fees to be paid, when it is due, and how it is to be paid. Consider including your payment method as well as any fees related to late payments or check bounces.

Deposits and Additional Fees. Be clear on what you may use the deposit for (damages, overdue bills, cleaning fees) as well as what the tenant is not allowed to use the deposit for (final month's rent). It is also beneficial to include where the deposit is being held, and whether it will accrue any interest.

Damage and Maintenance. Make sure the responsibilities of both the tenant and yourself are well documented in this section so that both yourself and the tenant know where they stand in this regard. Include any restrictions on the tenant altering the property that you would like.

Pets. All restrictions and conditions on pets must be placed here.

Once you are well set and organized, you can begin to advertise your property. Since there is a massive demand for property, you will most definitely receive offers for your property once it is out there. Placing advertisements on social media, property websites, as well as more wholesale websites will all bring prospective tenants straight to you.

As I said in the beginning, this is one of the more straightforward methods of bringing in a passive income, and can be one of the most reliable. It can provide a more stable footing for you to go out and live comfortably.

Chapter 9: Cryptocurrency

The cryptocurrency market has seen massive growth in recent times. You've probably heard bits and pieces about it around the news and maybe from some of your friends.

One of the biggest names in cryptocurrency being Bitcoin, had you invested $100 in Bitcoin in 2011, that investment would have soared to over a million dollars in 2019. In 2017 alone, Bitcoin saw an approximate increase of around 1500%, while another in Ethereum soared to over 10,000%. This just shows the ludicrously dramatic increase that has surged around cryptocurrency. While Bitcoin and a few others have undergone a bit of a rollercoaster ride in recent times, there is no doubt that cryptocurrency is still a great solution to earning additional income for yourself.

If you're still scratching your head to understand what is cryptocurrency, let me explain.

Cryptocurrency is a form of digital currency that conducts financial transactions to make money. This is usually done using cryptography, which is the science of hiding information. Cryptocurrency is entirely independent from government or individual control, which is completely unlike the banks and the money we use today.

Each cryptocurrency works through a ledger; a list of transactions that is shared by everyone, usually in the form of a blockchain. Now, a blockchain is the method of storing a list of entries, which cannot be changed easily once they have been created. This ledger serves as a database of all public transactions. Since the first inception, over 4000 cryptocurrencies have been created. Due to their independence, cryptocurrencies generally have their own interest rates and are not subject to the general rules of inflation or deflation (Blockgeeks, 2019).

Now, although there seems to be a lot of complications around cryptocurrencies, I hope I simplified it enough to give you a general idea of what it is as a market. In reality, it is just a selection of entries in a database that cannot be changed without certain criteria being met. In itself, cryptocurrency has no value.

With a logical mindset, and the right amount of research, you can become a legitimate success in the world of cryptocurrency.

Investing In Cryptocurrency

If you've chosen cryptocurrency to act as your passive income, then there is going to be a steep learning curve you're going to have to master before you start. Extensive research into how the process works, and what steps you need to take to develop your income are of utmost importance. Going in blind will could see you losing all the value you have consistently, so it is important that we minimize risks. Use simulators that work on the real time values to help you get ahead on the learning curve.

The necessary tools

Next, you're going to need to open up a few accounts, with the first being Coinbase. Coinbase will allow you to exchange your cash into cryptocurrency for you to invest with. You could consider using another exchange service, however this is what I find to be the most reliable and secure.

From there, you can set up a purchase for whatever cryptocurrencies you would like to purchase, at the amount you want to invest. Avoid the smaller cryptocurrency companies, as you will be more likely to fall victim to scams on any one of those. Here, it is best to stick with the top providers in the market.

While deciding how much you would like to invest, I would suggest that your initial investment be around 30% of your total investment value. What that means is that you should only invest a small portion of the total amount you have with which to invest, just to get you started, and to ensure you don't have a big loss. The amount of your initial investment must be an amount that you are comfortable with making a loss on, should that occur.

Once you have purchased your chosen currencies, you will need a place to keep them safe. This is called a wallet. You can choose to either have a software wallet or a hardware wallet. Hardware wallets are used in a similar manner to external hard drives. These can be used when you don't plan on accessing currencies anytime soon. On the other hand, software wallets are used when you want to be active in your trading.

Be sure to diversify your portfolio. As you would with regular investments, don't throw all your eggs in one basket. Diversifying your portfolio will help to shield you when currencies become extremely volatile, and help to protect you from overall losses.

Stay clear of mobile wallets, as these tend to be a bit on the suspicious side, and are not as secure as software or hardware wallets.

From there, you're ready to trade. How you choose to trade is purely up to you and your strategy. You could choose to be really aggressive, and go for short term gains, or play the long term game with your investment. The choice is yours.

A Bit Of A Heads Up

Prepare yourself for this type of market, should you choose to invest in it. Cryptos are excessively volatile. A gain five minutes ago could turn into severe losses an hour later. You need to steel yourself to these occurrences, and ensure that you don't act out on rash decision-making and emotions. This is why it is so important to only invest as much as you can afford to lose.

As I've already mentioned, but will mention again; stick with the more reliable cryptocurrency providers. Due to the difficult and independent nature of cryptocurrencies, it can be very easy to get caught up in a scam. You need to be aware what are the signs that something isn't right, and when to move away.

Make sure that you have a reason to enter each trade. Trading impulsively could see you losing at a constant rate. Did you see a pattern? Something that made you consider buying in? Make sure that every investment has a reason behind it.

With that being said, avoid buying simply because the price is low. This is a mistake several newbies make. If they see a drop in price, they will buy in, assuming it's cheaper and will rise in value at some point.

Finally, set goals for yourself. It may sound a bit strange when dealing with such a volatile market, however setting goals will help you establish a medium of what you aim to achieve. Given we're looking at passive income, this could be a target for you to reach each month. However, in this case you will need to be flexible in your goals, to accommodate the volatility.

While you may balk at the amount of risk involved in cryptocurrency, time has proven that there are many ways to minimize that risk and in turn collect huge rewards. In fact, I would say that cryptocurrency has the potential to deal out the largest profits. However, as with all investments, big rewards require big risks. That doesn't mean you can't play it safe. Evaluate what type of trader you want to be and what are the best platforms for you to exercise your strategy and achieve your goals. Remember, the most successful investors will always remain calm in the face of adversity, as they know that another opportunity will always present itself. Emotional traders will always be losing trades, so learn to trade objectively instead, and in time you will reap the benefits of your consistency.

Chapter 10: Google Adsense

If you think about, advertisements have been around for as long as one can remember. They have been the number one way for businesses to promote themselves and their product. As time has continued, ads have remained, but only the medium has changed. Now you could probably find ads in just about every place imaginable, especially in the online market. Just about every website has a few ads here and there, and only a select few claim to be completely ad-free. This could mean that we tons of random ads on varying sites that hold no relevance. That is where Google Adsense comes into play.

Now this is something I mentioned a little earlier when discussing ways of creating income from a blogging site. Google Adsense displays ads on your website that are relatable to the content that you have, as well as based on previous user searches. Once users start clicking those ads, you will receive payment as Adsense works on a system of cost-per-click and shared revenue. What this means is that you will want as many users as possible to click on those ads.

From these clicks you will generally receive a commission cut ranging from anywhere between 20 cents to a couple dollars. Remember, this is earned at a cost per click, so generating a high rate of clicks could grant you a substantial increase in revenue.

It is estimated that around 10 million websites are now using Google Adsense. They provide security and transparency for both the advertisers and publishers. Google makes sure that both sides have a clear understanding of the whole process and everything can be tracked.

On top of this, Adsense is capable of running a variety of formats for its ads. You can run your ads in text, image, video and several others as well. This gives freedom of experimentation to better suit your website.

Google Adsense will also give you the option to block ads that rival your content. This is a handy feature when you find that the ads you are promoting are taking sales away from you and handing it to your competitors.

Using Google Adsense To Make You Money

So now that we've established that Google Adsense can be a source of income, it's time to determine how you can go about doing it. This doesn't involve throwing ads on your website, sitting back and the money will miraculously roll in. You need to invest your time into making it profitable so that you can generate a return.

For starters, you're going to need a website or a blog. As we looked at previously, you're going to need to focus on a niche that you can center these ads around.

When applying for a Google Adsense account, there is going to be a few criteria that you have to consider:

Ensure you own the Domain. Part of the process of your application will require you to verify ownership of your domain. If you can't verify that you own the domain, then Google will reject your application.

Quality Content. We looked at this throughout this book, so I imagine it is no surprise that to be considered, you need to have quality content. This also does not mean you can develop high quality content, and tail off once you pick up some ads. Google will remove your account if they deem your content to not be up to scratch. This is why it is important to consider a passion as your source for a niche. You will be inspired and driven to deliver something interesting and meaningful if you care about it.

The Age of your site. This one is fairly new from Google. You will now be required to own your site and post content for at least six months before you apply for Adsense.

Google Policies and standards. Make sure that your website adheres to all the policies that Google sets forth, as well as their standards and restrictions on certain content.

While this seems like a lot to consider, it is only because Google wants to provide the best content with remuneration and ensure that everything is moderately regulated.

Optimizing The Ad Experience

Once you've passed Google's criteria, you're going to need to make sure that your ads are positioned optimally to generate more clicks. This will center around how you display ads alongside your content. Make sure that they compliment each other; your content will still take preference, but the ads should still stand out.

Consider setting up your ads alongside a Call to Action (CTA). A CTA is a technique that instructs users to perform a particular action on your site. Since CTAs are designed to draw attention to themselves, placing ads around them could potentially draw attention to the ads as well.

Now we get to what I would consider a bit of a hiccup. Adblock tools. As we find ads in more places around the internet, more users are turning to adblock to restrict ads from appearing, so they can focus solely on content. Unfortunately, there isn't much way around this. All you could do is simply ask them in a polite manner, to turn their adblock off. A study revealed that more people would be willing to turn off their adblock feature if you simply asked them to.

Something else to take into note, is the potential amount of mobile users you may have. Smartphones are everywhere, and you would be making quite an error if you chose not to cater to this market. You will need to adjust your site to become not only more mobile-friendly, but you will have to adjust the ads as well to cater to that audience.

Taking your income further

Ideally, if you feel that Adsense is not enough for you, you could opt to increase your earnings by combining with another form of passive income. Affiliate marketing could be a great supplement to the revenue you generate from Adsense. You could also decide to sell your own products and services as well. At the end of the day, it really is up to you how you choose to run your business. Although each of these chapters focuses on one aspect of passive income, you could combine as many as you would like, as long as it is effective and caters to your lifestyle.

While Google Adsense does seem a bit on the stricter side, they are generally asking for what most online providers ask for these days: consistency, suitability and relevance. Making sure you are up to date with their policies and providing quality content should generally be a norm on any platform you use, and so I'm sure that you will grow accustomed to it in no time.

Google Adsense provides a great opportunity to earn income while focusing your time on other income opportunities. Take the opportunity!

Chapter 11: Online Courses

The constant surges in technology have not only given way to increases in advertising and marketing strategies. They have given way to the potential for learning as well. These days, you could probably learn just about anything you want online. From mathematics to programming to the complexities of a cell. All of it is at the touch of your fingertips.

Likely, in such a market, there is always the opportunity to be seized, and creating online courses is one way you could go about it. Creating your own online courses provides you with the chance to share your expertise with others in a constructive manner. As the industry grows, there are several companies capitalizing on the market, hosting entire websites devoted to a variety of topics for prospective learners to access.

It is estimated that around 33 percent of students have taken online courses, however this does not include those who have chosen to learn later in life. Online courses are not just about professional skills and student-based subjects. It can be about anything that you have a talent for or experience in doing. Online courses can be about anything from cooking to writing, to painting tutorials and maybe even lessons on how to be a decent clown performer. Anything really means anything.

The benefits to online learning can be immense, as a learner has the potential to receive a wide variety of teaching methods, such as video and audio content, in order to grasp the concepts of what they are learning. Whereas before, it's well-known that anyone who did a bit of self-learning usually looked at the old-fashioned textbook. Online courses have reinvigorated learning to make it a much more fun and interesting experience.

Creating Your Own Online Courses

Creating your own course is actually somewhat similar to starting up a blog at the beginning. It's funny how all these different options tend to intertwine. As you would pick a niche for your blog that you have an interest in, you would choose a course topic that you are most passionate about. Your training will come off as dull if you decide to engage with a topic you couldn't care less about. However, you will also need to consider the demand for your course. You'll feel rather frustrated if you're creating all these online courses and there's nobody willing to buy them.

Look for gaps in the competition that match your skill sets and experience, to ensure that you are entering a market that is demanding your knowledge. Try to find something that sets you apart from the other course creators in your field. What makes your courses more interesting and exciting than theirs?

Include course outcomes

A key aspect of course creation is to make sure all your courses have course outcomes. It wouldn't be a good idea to hand a course to a learner, and they have no idea what it is they are supposed to be achieving. Students will most likely want to know how your course is going to help them, and if this isn't provided, they may not want to enrol in your course.

The purpose of the learning outcome is to ensure that learners will have a clear understanding of what they will be able to accomplish once they have completed each section of the course, as well as by the end of the course. It should describe the skills they have learned and the knowledge they have gained from completing this course. This will also lead to fewer cases of unhappiness amongst students and fewer refunds to boot.

Plan your content

Once you have outlined what the course is going to achieve, you need to plan the content of your course. Given that this is a field of your talent and expertise, you may be inclined to push the envelope a little too far on what you include. Therefore, instead of considering what you need to include, consider what you need to leave out. This is where the learning outcomes will play a role for you. Anything that is not directly related to the learning outcomes should be removed altogether.

All this content will then need to be ordered into modules and organized. You will need to group all the similar content, tips and ideas together in each of their respective modules, so that the learning is flowing and progressive.

Your course should follow a natural and logical progression in the learning phase.

Teaching methods

Now that all your material is grouped together and organized into a structured course, you need to determine your method of delivery. You will need to be considerate of who it is that you are targeting with your content. Are they adults or children? Both? Consider the various ways you can deliver your course, so that it remains interesting for all of the potential learners you may have. Your method of deliver can include video, audio, reading and exercises to best enhance the learning experience. Try to strike a balance between all of these methods, to keep your learners engaged throughout the course.

Now comes the interesting part! You need to get on camera! Okay, well maybe you don't **need** to, but it is proven that the best way to deliver learning is through video. If you don't feel like getting on camera, you could use screencasting instead. Screencasting is when you display a recording of your screen for video. This way, you can do a voiceover, along with an on-screen tutorial, while you don't have anyone seeing your face.

If you don't want to include a video tutorial at all then that is fine, but consider that you want to maximize your potential for profits as much as possible, and the most effective online learning method will help see to that. (Edition, 2019)

Selling And Marketing Your Course

The course is now complete, and you are ready to have students take your skills and knowledge on board. In order to do that, you need to decide how you're going to sell your online courses. Three of the more legitimate ways to sell your course is through learning management systems, online course marketplaces or through your very own website.

A learning management system (LMS) is basically like having your own little academy, and will function as your very own brand. On the other hand, an online course marketplace is a platform where anybody is allowed to sell online courses on the same site. These sites usually do not keep track or analyse the courses before sales, so a course can be anything from extremely high quality and informative, to extremely low quality and just plain dreadful. You website is, well; it's your website. This decision is really up to you.

Another crucial decision that will be in your hands is the pricing of your courses. Look at your potential competitors to see what they are charging for a similar product. Now comes the controversial part. Consider pricing yours slightly higher than theirs. Why? Well a lower course price will make customers feel like it is of a lower quality, and that will work against you rather than with you.

Now you're probably ready to sell your product, but you need customers. It's back to the good old marketing strategies for you! Even if your course is completed, how are people going to find out much about it?

One thing to consider is to partner up with an influencer who creates content that is relevant to your own. Reach out to various influencers and find out who is willing to market your products.

Make sure that you are always one step ahead in your marketing strategies. This means planning out the strategies you will undertake as time progresses. As the course creator, and the most knowledgeable on the matter, you will know where it is you will find students for your course. With that in mind, I'm sure you've already pinpointed a few places where you could potential market your course. Social media, once again, will be your friend.

Make sure to persuade any students you do receive to sign up for email notifications, so that you can inform them when you do have another course being rolled out, especially when it all falls under one ongoing subject.

And there you have it. Online courses provide the perfect opportunity to share your wealth of skills with the world, developing and earning a profit while helping others to pick up new skills themselves. Pretty nifty, don't you think?

Chapter 12: AirBnB Business

Traveling is something that we would like to do or that we all love to do. Generally, I imagine every one of us would leap on board the opportunity to travel were we given the chance. However, the sad truth is that for many of us, the costs involved are just too great. From flights, to hotels, to food and drinks, there are so many expenses that we have to consider. However, Airbnbs have come about to help alleviate some of these costs.

Airbnb is an online marketplace where travelers can find hosts to book space in various accommodations around the world. If you're interested in the term, Airbnb comes from air mattress B&B, where B&B stands for bed and breakfast. Airbnbs provide travelers with an incredibly expansive list of options for accommodation, at a much cheaper rate than you would pay to stay at a hotel. This also provides the chance for travelers to "live like a local", enhancing their overall experience.

All that you would do is list your property on the website, and then wait for reservations. Given these are short term rentals, you may be a bit on the fence about whether to opt for a longer term standard rental or an Airbnb. However, short term stays can be beneficial in their own right. You get to enjoy having new guests and meeting new and exciting people every few days. This can provide you with an opportunity to experience and interact with a variety of people from different cultures while presenting your own cultures to them.

You'll also have the option to be flexible in your pricing. Airbnb allows you to change your price listing as often as you'd like, should you wish to. With all this in mind, should you have a property that you have available, that you would like to rent out, consider using Airbnb to provide future travelers with a comfortable home from home.

Setting Up An AirBnB

First things first. Make sure you're acquainted with the laws in your area. There are some places where Airbnb hosting is banned, while in others, it is regulated. Make sure you are extremely knowledgeable about the regulations in your area so that you can avoid any serious troubles later on.

Decide your hosting calendar

You will need to decide how often a year you would like to host. Airbnb allows you to set the dates and months you would like to be available for hosting as well as the maximum or minimum permitted time that a guest is allowed to stay.

Security

Although Airbnb provides their own assurances when it comes to damages, consider taking out insurance on special items in your home that are not covered by Airbnb's guarantee. This will give you peace of mind if any rowdy occupiers end up causing damage to your home. To partially circumvent these kinds of problems, consider the type of traveler you would like to appeal to. Is your property located close to the business district? If so, consider targeting business travelers who have an agenda within the district. Always look to appeal to the market you want.

Knowing and exceeding the competition

Make sure that you know what Airbnbs are around the same area as you as they will likely be your main competition. Research their properties to determine where you can receive an edge in the market to push yourself above them in demand from travelers. Make sure your property is clean and well maintained, so that it can decorated into something extremely appealing to your guests.

Make sure that you have the amenities that are essential to your guest's needs as well as those that deliver a wonderful experience. Try to invest a bit in stylish furniture and artwork to make your property more vibrant and interesting. Guests will always go for the property that is pleasing on the eyes, and so it is integral to maintain just that.

Your Airbnb Profile

Your profile with Airbnb is arguably going to be the most important feature of your business. As customers will not be able to pay a visit to check out your property, they will rely on the information you gave about the listing to determine if it is suitable.

You will need to set up your home type, location, whether they will rent the "Entire place," or will they be a part of a group of shared guests? Make sure you know exactly how many guests your property can accommodate in total. Any form of overbooking can lead to all sorts of problems, and none of them are where you will come out on top.

Next, you will need to set up the actual profile of your property. This is more or less advertising your property to potential tenants.

Make sure you have snapped some professional photos of the different areas of the home to show off on the page. Try to take pictures where a room is cast in light, and looks masterful in presentation. The better the pictures, then more people will be keen to stay on your premises. Show off the different rooms, amenities and other features that are unique to your property.

Potential guests will also be interested in the description that you provide, as this needs to paint a portrait of how exciting and interesting your property is. Try to include a bit of your personality in your description, in order to make your property shine. Avoid writing too much, as this will become a bit exhausting to read. Use short sentences and bullet points so that you are emphasizing your points.

Once you have uploaded pictures and completed your description, make sure to list all the amenities that your property has. I mean **all** of them. There are many features that people will look for, and some are more specific than others. These could be that make or break that determines whether a traveler opts for your property instead of another.

One thing to do to help your guests is offer extra services, such as transport from the airport for an added fee. Given they are in a new location, this might be a welcome addition for those who have just hopped off a plane and can think of nothing better than to have a decent sleep as soon as possible.

Once your guests have arrived, make sure to greet them and provide them with a tour of where they will be staying. Give them a rundown of the area, and suggest some attractions for them to potentially visit. Make sure that your guests feel well-treated, and try to be on hand to provide assistance as much as possible. Do your utmost to make any guests feel at home during your stay. Why? Well, Airbnb includes a review service on their website, which is also a part of your property listing. In a world where there is much uncertainty, having decent reviews can be the difference between a traveler deciding between a competitor and yourself. If you have the better, more consistent reviews, then these clients will be more likely to stay on your property instead. Treat the moment as an experience to learn about someone new. This way, you will be more eager to help them with anything they may need, and they will most definitely be more willing to engage with you.

While Airbnb is not one of those markets with unlimited potential, it provides an ideal option for those looking to gain something of a second salary for several parts of the year, in order to better their financial position.

Chapter 13: Dividend Investments

Let's look at some of the more well-known methods that we see being used all the time. Now, most people see stocks as this terribly toxic monster that they never want to venture anywhere near. Others spot opportunities to make money. Those who are too fearful simply do not spot the chances available to them to grow their money. They fail to spot that there could potentially a agap to increase their earnings, without suffering huge losses. Dividend Investing is one of those opportunities.

Unlike other investments, dividend stocks are stocks that allow you to generate a steady stream of income. The purpose here is to build short term income, while setting up long term wealth. How does this work? Well, the idea is that you would invest in a company that pays out dividends during the course of the year. That could range from every few months to twice a year. Dividends are the monies paid out to shareholders out of a company's profits (My Accounting Course, 2019).

This allows you to create a steady income stream during the course of a year, while your wealth generates over a longer term. As that term increases, so do your potential payouts. Most consumers ideally want shorter term rewards, and dividend stocks provides an opportunity for those to occur.

Although stocks inherently carry risks, with extensive research you can learn how the best traders operate so that you can minimize your own risks and receive constant reward.

Investing In Dividend Stocks

When it comes to stocks, you're going to need to do extensive research into the trade. You need to learn how to read the stocks, spot trends, use the tools and several other factors that will govern your role as a successful stock investor.

Have an investment strategy

Going in, you will need to have a strategy on how you choose to invest. Determine how you're going to generate better long term returns. Given you will still generate dividends over the year, your goal will always be to find the best long term stock options.

What to look for in stocks

Don't buy stocks simply for the sake of dividends is a crucial error that many investors can make when starting out. You may find a company has a high dividend yield, however their stock is falling dramatically. Include the potential taxes in this, and you will simply be at a standstill or begin making losses on your investment. On top of that, it is unwise to simply invest in high-dividend stocks, as these could be a sign of problems within the business or low future growth. This will damage any long term investments you will make.

Payout Ratios

Look for important numbers such as **The Payout Ratio**. The Payout Ratio is the amount of earnings that is paid out to shareholders, expressed as a percentage. There is no ideal payout ratio, however this ratio can help you in determining a few factors about a company. For example, if a company's payout ratio is fairly high, say around 58% or higher, you may find that this is a sign that this company is issuing too many of their earnings to shareholders.

On the opposite side, a company with lower payout ratio may be related to low performance. At the same time, a company with high payout ratios but low performance have seen their earnings fall over time, but the dividends remain the same. Dividends that pay less than 50% with signs that the rest is going back into the business will bring about future growth.

You need to consider a company's overall track record over a number of years in order to assess whether they are a healthy option to invest in. A company with healthy growth and strong payout ratio may be a fantastic opportunity to invest.

Dividend Yield

The next aspect you will need to consider is the dividend yield. This is the return you will receive from your investment in the form of payments. However, there are key indicators you will need to watch out for. For example, if the dividend yield goes up, it could be a result of falling stock. A fairly normal dividend yield should be considered between 2% and 6%.

Consistency

This is one of the most important aspects when looking at dividend stocks. Think of it as the credit record of a stock. You'll want to be looking for companies that have been consistent in raising their dividend payments, or have generally kept these payments the same over a number of years, no less than three.

Picking individual stocks is a tough business, so it's imperative to ensure that you know what you are doing, especially since most of us don't. One thing to consider is that you are trying to secure an income. While there may be others with cash to burn, looking to make high risk manoeuvres in the market, you're trying to protect your money and attain a reasonable safety net.

Look for companies that have high returns on equity, with little to no debt. These are signals that the business is of fairly good standing, and could provide a good cushion should anything problematic occur.

Dividend investing, like most stock trades, is mostly about predicting the future possibilities and standings of a business. Predicting correctly can lead to consistent returns and increased income and stock value, so that you can build an income that you can not only live comfortably on, but at the very end, you can receive value from the stocks you spent years accumulating, which could end up being a nice retirement treat.

A Few Suggestions

You're going to want to **pay attention to the companies that pay these dividends**. It's not just about the finances involved and their credibility. Look at whether it is a company that you want to invest in. Consider the business model as well. The way a company is run can tell you a lot about its future prospects. Consider yourself as part of this company. You're a shareholder, so get to know it!

Learn how to **use dividend yields to tell if a stock is overvalued or undervalued**. This can tell you a bit about the current trajectory of the stock market and its potential trends. Learn a few methods to determine this, so that you can understand the risks that you take when purchasing a stock.

You can **use your dividends to help you recover from your losses**. If you took a big hit in the value of your investments, you may want to use your dividends to reinvest and rebuild over the next period of time. This will help you to ensure longer term stability.

Diversify your stocks. As you would with cryptocurrency, diversifying your stock profile will help to provide a safety blanket should one of your investments fall. Never hedge your bets all on just a few stock options.

Try to invest in sectors and markets you understand. Ah, the niche argument. Try to invest in places that you are knowledgeable about. For example, you may end up investing in a market that is in severe decline, but you don't know that because you know nothing about the sector. This could all have effects on any stock you may have.

While it is clear that stock trading is not for everyone, the potential that exists within this market is fantastic, and could earn you wonderful rewards in your lifetime.

Chapter 14: Forex Trading

All around the world, we have several different currencies that we use. The US has the dollar, Britain the Pound, and most of Europe uses the Euro. Several other countries and continents have their own currencies as well. None of these currencies really have the same value, as each one is affected differently by factors such as inflation. These factors determine the prices of each currency in relation to another. In the current market, it is possible to take advantage of these factors. This is where Forex trading features. Short for foreign exchange, it is a network of buyers and sellers of currency, who transfer these currencies between each other at an agreed price. If you have ever traveled abroad, you most likely have used forex to exchange currency.

Given that currencies rise and fall in value, we can use this knowledge to earn a profit. Every day, the prices of currencies are moving, which is what is so attractive to most traders. While there is an increased risk, the chance for profits can be very high. Forex trading allows you to bet on how you assume the markets are likely to move. The idea is that you buy a currency pair, when you believe that the base currency will strengthen against its opposite currency. Or you could choose to sell a currency pair if you believe that the base currency is expected to weaken against the opposite currency.

There are several benefits to trading in forex. For one, the market is open 24 hours a day, 5 days a week, from Sunday night when the markets open right up until Friday night when the markets close again. The forex market is extremely volatile, which paves the way for larger profit margins in trading. Forex also provides several risk management tools that you can use to minimize your losses when you need to. These include stop losses, price alerts, running balances and many more. As with the general stock market, you will have a wide variety of optional currencies available for you to trade in. There are over 80 currency pairs that you can choose from; from the major currencies to minor and emerging pairs, all traded in the same place.

While the forex market is seen as higher risk than stocks due to its volatility, it is still the more popular of the two markets, and allows for much greater flexibility in gathering rewards over both the longer and shorter terms.

Trading in Forex

If Forex is the route you wish to undertake, you're going to have to read up on some of the terms and research how the currencies work. Entering a field where you don't understand any of terms being thrown at you will leave you a little bamboozled when you see them. So here are a few that you may see quite often:

Base currency. If you were scratching your head when I mentioned this earlier, then allow me to explain. Base currency is simply the currency that you are currently holding. Usually this is dependent on the country that you are in.

Quote currency. The currency that you will purchase.

Spread. This is the difference between the bidding price and the asking price.

Bidding price. This is the price that your broker is willing to buy your base currency for.

Asking price. This is the price that your broker will ask for when you are buying a quote currency. Once you have learned a few of the terms used, you can do some research on the market without spending the time being entirely confused.

Choosing your broker Once you're getting started, and you know that you want to invest in forex, you will need to find your own broker. Choose a well known and credible brokerage company, as this could have a big difference on your overall future trade success. Look up reviews and info about the best brokerage firms available.

Learn more about the world Research the political spectrums, GPDs, news and trading positions of the countries you are interested in. This will help you find economies with potential growth, and which countries you should potentially stay away from.

Start trading Now that you've got a secure enough knowledge to begin trading, it is time to make your first trade. Choose your currencies, determine the variables and then sit back and let your broker handle the next phases.

Trading Successfully

Once you have started trading and you're familiar with the market, you need to begin honing your skills to make forex trading successful enough to be considered a passive income.

Stick to the plan

One problem that many new traders may feel is the fear of losing. They may buy into a currency, but then choose to opt out if there is a slight turn against them. The key here is to have a plan when you're going in and stick to it.

Set the parameters to ensure you have security in place and then let it run. Only make trades that fall within your plan. It is usually said that you make rational decisions before the trade and irrational decisions after the trade has been made.

Know your limits

Unlike the common gambler, know when enough is enough. Know how much you are willing to take a risk on for each trade, and don't push above them. If you're making a loss, don't begin investing in other currencies in the hope of balancing them. You will lose full control over your trading.

This includes knowing when to stop a trade. Utilize the stop and limit orders you have at your disposal to reach your targets with your trades, or prevent too much decline.

Calculate the success of your system

As a trader, you will need to have a process that you follow with all your trades. However, this should not be followed blindly whether you win or lose. Calculate your success by working out the average success of each trade, as well as the average profit of loss you make from each. While it is important to be consistent in your approach, if that approach is not working, you will need to reevaluate your system and see how you can improve.

Only spend what you can afford to lose

I've mentioned this before, but I'll mention it again to make sure. Do not spend money that you've reserved for household purposes or savings. Only use money that will not harm you in any way, should you lose it. As you are developing this as a passive income, you will need to play the long game, prioritizing stable income over short term reward.

Based on the information above, some would be inclined to think that forex is an easier market to get into, however this is not the case. Your learning curve will be a steep one if you believe that forex can be used as a get rich scheme. Instead, play it slow and you will reap the benefits of your growing experience.

Chapter 15: Swing Trading

As you have gathered, trading can be a highly successful industry for the average passive income seeker. There are several different options to explore to suit your needs and swing trading is one of these. Swing trading has begun to receive an ever growing number of new traders in the market, with more and more people becoming aware of it as an alternative. Day trading is the buying and selling of stocks within a single day. Each day is a new start and nothing carries over. Swing trading is more or less the same thing, however you will hold on to stocks for days to weeks before selling them. Swing trading is a form of active, short term investments (Investinganswers.com, 2019). In more basic terms, swing trading is the act of buying low and selling high.

The premise is that you will buy a stock based on an indicator determining whether there will be an upward or downward trend in the near future. This completely ignores the long term values of stock, prioritizing short term gains. This makes swing trading a high-risk strategy, as because its focus is on the quick stock gains, it is more vulnerable to economic downturns. However, the process for swing training is extensively simplified, meaning you can rely on technical indicators alone when making your trades.

Swing trading is useful to those who have some free time to work around their full time jobs or for students to make some extra cash, as it in no way requires the length of time you would spend on day trading. In general, swing trading will take up approximately 45 minutes of your time. This also gives you time to consider other forms of developing your income. Choosing the right trading platform for you should all be about the personality that you have. Choosing a platform that is against your personality will make you lose the sense of excitement you receive from making trades. Find what caters to your behaviors before jumping on board, so that you are happy with the path you've chosen.

Swing Trading As Income

Investment capital

Although there is no minimum recommended amount, the recommended amount for swing traders to invest is $1,500. This is to ensure that you have sufficient capital to invest in a few trades at the start.

Risk management strategies

Before you get started, as with all trades, you need to limit the amount of risk that comes with the trading. This can be done with a risk management strategy. This will provide an organized and reasonable approach to managing and identifying risks as they come. Being inconsiderate of the risks imposed could be detrimental to your overall stock venture, and could see you stop before you even get started.

What stocks will you trade

One of the things you will need to learn is how to pick the right stocks. Research videos and guides on how to find and pick the right sticks for your needs. Choosing the stock picks is the basis of your swing strategy. Your strategy will be useless if you continue to pick the wrong stocks. A general rule to consider is that large-cap stocks will often have the levels of volume and volatility you need.These stocks will have higher highs and lower lows. Large-cap stocks are the shares of well-known companies that you often see on the news. These companies generally have a market capitalization of more than $5 billion.

Trade in the right markets

To swing trade successfully, you will need to trade in the right markets, at the right times. You will be aware of the fact that there are two market extremes:

Bear market. A bear market is when the stock market is characterized by falling prices and are typically shrouded in negativity.

Bull market. A bull market is the opposite. A bull market shows rising prices and expectations that they will rise even further. Bull markets usually take place when an economy is growing stronger.

Essentially, for you then, you will find that the optimum time to swing trade is in a period when the markets aren't actually heading anywhere. This can be constituted by a repeating pattern in the market.

Consider using a swing trading academy or tutorial to help you practice.

The given saying is that practice makes perfect. A decent academy will run you through the various indicators, alerts and other tools you will need to make your swing trading venture a meaningful one.

Setting Up For the Rewards

One of the aspects of stock trading that is not often mentioned, is the psychology of trading. There is no guide or instruction telling you how to react when things don't go your way, or even for that matter when they are going your way. Knowing how to react to the situation can spell the difference between suffering a substantial loss, or breaking even if it hasn't been a good time in the trades. The idea is not that you need to be fearless. You should fear losing your money. That will make you more careful with it. It is how you choose to combat these feelings and effects with your thinking.

For example, you can **lessen your fear by reducing the risks**. As I said before, everybody's strategy is different, and some may decide to risk more than others. Therefore, you need to determine what works for you, by setting your own limits for yourself and sticking to them.

Although swing trading is considered a form of short term trading; in the world of day trading, it is considered to be a long term trade. As time goes on during these trades, and they start to make a loss for a short period, some investors will begin to panic thinking everything has turned against them. Do not take these losses personally, and instead, **prioritize the long term** profits that you foresaw when you purchased the stock.

Most importantly, in any venture, **never stop learning**. As you journey through, you can end up picking up new skills and techniques that drive you from one income standpoint to the next and so forth, finding ways to get the most out of your investments. Those who stop learning will usually fall behind in the markets, and struggle to keep up with the investors who treat learning their field as a hobby. They love the markets, so they crave to learn more all the time.

The amount of money to be made is entirely dependent on you. Your strategy as a stock investor and the techniques that you use will determine how far your passive income can reach. If it is your first time trading, then swing trading is a great option for beginners to start learning and honing their skills before moving on to more complex forays into the stock market.

Although the hiccup is that you will need a bit of capital, this is to ensure that you stand a greater chance of making a profit in the market, rather than stagnating with a smaller amount. With all this at your disposal, you will find your venture into the stock markets can be quite an interesting and exciting one!

Chapter 16: Personal Brand

Personal branding. I am sure that for many, this is as confusing as it gets. Simply put, your personal brand is how you promote yourself. You are showing off the unique skills and personality that you have for the world to see. In a professional setting, your personal brand is the image that people see of you. It relies on a combination of social media presence, as well as your image in real life. In many ways, personal branding helps to build trust between people.

People are generally more comfortable when they are able to understand what another person's capabilities are. Personal branding helps you to build connections and establish credibility with others. In your area of specialty, having the right connections in the right places helps you to build a reputation, and will improve your ability to gain exposure. Others will see you as an expert in your field and will respect and acknowledge you for it. On a personal note, personal branding can be extremely empowering, helping you to gain confidence and motivation to achieve more.

Yes, yes, I know what you are asking. How does this help you make any passive income? Well, I'm getting there. Personal branding in a more broader term is the process of marketing people and their career as a brand. Well, a personal brand gives you the opportunity to market the products or services you have even further. Think of it this way. If you had a product right now, that you were keen to get on the market, you'd need to attract a customer base. In the case of personal branding, you already have a following who are in tune with what you are offering. Having a personal brand shows what sets you apart from the others within your niche, and shows people who they will potentially be doing business with. Your personal brand streamlines the process it takes to drive your success and takes you even further in the long run.

Creating Your Own Personal Brand

If you want to build your personal brand, you're going to need to understand that you have to put yourself out there; to be seen in the public eye, whether on social media or in reality. People don't do business with companies anymore. They do business with people they like, based on relationships, connections and trust. However, it may still be the early stages for you and we need to start at the basics. Results will also not come straight away. Creating a personal brand will take some time before you start seeing any results. When starting off, there are a few things to consider to get yourself off the ground:

Blogging

Already mentioned earlier, but in the case of personal branding, consider setting up your own blog. Be consistent and blog about topics that are connected to your niche. Share your expertise, and be interactive with the audience members you do pick up to ensure they stick around to learn more about you. Make sure you know who your target customer is before proceeding any further, as this will define who you reach out to.

Guest Posting

Even if you do have your own blog, guest posting can be a great way to gain exposure on more popular platforms. Guest posting is when you are writing an article and publishing it on someone else's website or blog, allowing you to connect with a larger audience. This will help to grow your following, and from there push on to newer ventures.

Host events and be a speaker at conferences

Speaking at conferences, or perhaps even hosting an event can help you to build up your brand in a positive light, and place you and your company in the spotlight. The idea is that you want to use these opportunities to 'sell yourself' to the audience. Show them exactly why you are an expert in your field and know the purpose of your speech. It would help if you had a little understanding of who your audience is as well. This will help you in being able to engage with them. Audience engagement is vital, as this is making sure that your audience is fully tuned in to what you are saying. Think of a magician on stage, and how he shrouds the audience in mystery with his act. You will need to do something similar, using your words and the tools you have at your disposal.

Be active on social media

This is a given in today's world. Make sure that you are active on at least two social networks, and that LinkedIn is one of them to engage with more professional clients. There isn't much excuse for not being active on social media in today's time, and it will result in most people thinking you have something to hide. Even if that is not the case, people will be suspicious of someone who doesn't conform to the set standards. It is not for their interest that you will have social media, but for you to market your personal brand and your business online on the most popular platforms.

The digital world is not the only world

Although most of the ways we have looked at passive income as a whole have been digital, it is not the only way to go about things. As you develop your personal brand, consider potential clients when you are out and about, always keep business cards handy and dress in a professional manner. This will make sure that you're ready to always make a good impression, irrespective of the scenario. The personal brand is you, and so you have reflect that at all times.

Monetizing Your Personal Brand

All of these are ways to develop and enhance your personal brand. Obviously, to begin, you need to have a concept, a plan and an audience you are trying to reach. What we focused on was growing that audience. Now you need to turn a profit off of all this hard work you have been doing. Here you will need to consider the various methods we looked at previous and a few upcoming methods in order to grow your passive income.

Monetize your blog. As a personal brand, you may not want to just litter your blog in ads for profit. Consider courses and ebooks as a way that will further enhance your brand and that you can look to, in order to begin gaining an income.

Create an online community. If you have a sufficient enough audience, you could consider opening up a private community. However, as mentioned, you need to have enough users for this community to be able to run on its own. For this community, you can charge users a monthly subscription for access. If you're unsure if this is a good idea, ask your audience if this is something they would like to see. If there's enough interest then you have a new platform for an audience to communicate and grow from there.

Affiliate marketing. This is something we already know about. Your solid status as a personal brand will help your credibility when marketing products, as your audience are more trusting to what you may recommend. Ensure that the products and services you promote are of the highest quality before you promote them. Promoting and endorsing poor quality products can be detrimental to your brand and the trust the audience has in you.

As you can see, personal branding makes everything rather straightforward when building passive income. If you are consistent in your approach, then you could see your brand soar to completely new heights that you never expected, and revenues will soar with it! (Thimothy, 2019).

Chapter 17: Mobile App Development

In the current age, technology is increasing at an explosive rate. The demand for it is ever increasing as well, with more and more people gaining exposure to the world of technology. This is especially so in the case of smartphones. As we progress, the smartphone is becoming an absolute necessity for anyone living in the modern world.

With this demand for smartphones and handheld devices comes the demand for applications that meet every person's needs. It is estimated that over 5 billion people own a smartphone as of 2019, so it's only natural that this market should be considered for prospective app developers to get their hands into. Even if you're not a developer, you could take the time to learn the trade and consider making your own applications.

The industry ranges from individual developers to developers making applications for large companies. From here, you have the opportunity to involve yourself in an industry that is currently experiencing a growth surge at the moment. If you have a desire to solve problems and some creativity to match, then this is the market you should consider yourself getting into. For current developers, this is a fantastic opportunity to turn your passion into something greater.

Creating Your First App

If you have no prior experience in development, I trust that you know the first step is to get yourself acquainted with the industry. Start learning one of the most popular languages used for mobile, such as Java or Python. Practice creating test apps, or even cloning current ones as practice. Once you feel you're ready to build your first app, we can continue.

Conduct research Check out other apps, and see what sets them apart in the market. Consider their functionalities and what you could incorporate into your own app to make it more successful. Consider the various ways each app makes money on their product, as you will need this information when developing your app later. Search for gaps in the market where there is an opportunity for you to showcase an app.

Don't think big. At first Your first app should be nothing too extravagant. In fact, as you're new, it should be quite basic. This is merely the process of learning what it takes to create your own apps. The only purpose for your app for now, is that it should solve a problem. Why should it solve a problem? There will then be a demand for it. Once there is a demand for it, you can begin to market it.

Research the laws and regulations Before you begin creating your product, make sure it is in line with all laws and regulations related to a mobile application. GDPR (General Data Protection Regulation), AML (Anti Money Laundering) and KYC (Know Your Customer) are all integral with app development, and you will need to be familiar and knowledgeable of all of them if your app is to be successful.

Begin planning your app You should already have an idea of what you plan to create. Now you need to think about what features the app will have and what it will look like. Brainstorm ideas as to the general flow and layout of that. Remember that your app should be visually appealing, and user friendly. You can also plan out how each feature will work on your app, and the processes they will follow. This should include the navigation of certain functions and what will happen if a function is selected.

Start building your app. Once the planning is complete, you will then need to start building your app. To do that, you need the right software and tools. Try to research the best software and tools that will suit your needs. JIRA, GameSalad and Rollbar could be potential app creation software that suits your needs if you aren't too interested in learning to code. However, these are generally very basic, and are usually good enough for the first version of your app, but nothing further. Appy Pie is a potential option if you are keen on writing the code for the app yourself. It all depends on what your needs are and what you aim to achieve.

Test your app Almost every app needs to go through this testing phase. App testing is there to make sure the app works as it should, and there are no bugs or issues that will affect the user experience. Testing will also help you to find ways to make the app even better. You want to be able to develop the best app you possibly can. Pixate and Jasmine are potentially good app testing tools for you to get started with.

Release your app Once all the bugs have been ironed out and everything seems to be in order, you need to place your app somewhere that they can download and install it. The logical choice is with mobile app stores. The two monopolies in the industry being Apple and Google, you're going to want to get your product on their market. So how do we do this? Well, the processes are a bit different.

Google Playstore. Sign up to the Google Play Console and fill out the various details that outline your product. Google charges a one-time fee of $25 in order to create your developer account. Free apps don't cost anything, however Google takes 30% of the revenue for paid apps.

Apple Store. Apple prices are a little different as they charge an annual fee of $99 to all developers. With Apple, you will need to create an iOS distribution provisioning profile and distribution certificate. You can do this through another of Apple's platforms called Xcode. You will also need to set up your tax info as well as sign up for an iTunes Connect account. Once this is all completed, you can then follow the procedure towards adding an app to the store. Your app will then go for review and from there it's out of your hands. For now.

Monetization If your app is a paid product, then you've already monetized your product. However, if you haven't, you need to think about how you are going to do that. With mobile apps, there are several ways you can potentially create revenues towards a passive income:

In-app purchases. One of the many ways is through In-app purchases (IAPs). IAPs are options to purchase an added feature to the app to make it a more enjoyable experience. These generally don't hinder the overall experience of the product, as they are usually just for added visual effects.

Advertising. You could choose to display ads in your apps when users are connected to the internet. These ads can display at certain intervals during the app. If you choose this route, make sure that your app is not overloaded with apps that it ruins the user experience. You will also need to consider what types of ads you will be using (banners, display ads, videos).

Freemium products. These options are quite interesting. The idea is that your product is available for free, however free users will have certain restrictions on their account, that can be unlocked with paid content. This is usually of feature of mobile games, where a user can gain a competitive edge from paying for their content over other users who choose to remain free users.

Merchandise. If you have products that correspond with your app, you can consider advertising these on your app for anyone who would be interested in a potential purpose.

Sponsorship. Although probably the most difficult to attain, sponsorships can be a powerful tool for generating revenue from your app. This method can also benefit developers as they gain exposure to a greater audience.

There are several other ways to monetize your app as well, however the above have generally proven to be the most successful for the majority of app developers.

Marketing And Promotion

Now that your app is complete, you need to build your audience for the app. This will require a bit of work, as app stores have millions of apps and yours is amongst those millions just getting started. Without any sort of marketing, your app will potentially go unnoticed.

One thing you can do to combat this is to ensure that your app has great visuals that draw users to it on the app store. Make sure to include a detailed and interesting description along with a name that sounds catch and exciting.

Consider doing some general advertising of your product. This includes investing in ads on social media, Google and blogs as well.

Once again, another possibility could be for you to start a blog dedicated to your app. This can also provide a great platform for users to communicate with you directly and build an audience for future apps.

Earlier we mentioned that it is okay for the first version of your app to be a very basic version. However, from there, you will need to provide updates that improve the quality of the app and its content. If your app remains the same all the time, people will slowly grow bored and look for something better. It is up to you to make sure your audience remains engaged with your product.

Mobile App Development is most definitely a market where success can take you to the most incredible heights, given its tremendous demand. Even most success can be enough to build you a passive income that allows you to live freely, while performing something that brings you joy!

Chapter 18: YouTube Videos

It stands to reason that if you've not heard of YouTube by now, then it is possible that you've been living under a very big rock for a very long time. A very, very big rock.

In a world where the appeal of easily accessible visual content is becoming ever popular, YouTube has established itself as a mainstay in the market. In fact, YouTube is the largest video sharing platform of them all. YouTube provides an endless variety of content, from documentaries to movie trailers, music videos, educational videos, video blogging (vlogging), original video clips, game footage, live streams and many other aspects that you would like to include. Users on YouTube are allowed to share, like, subscribe and comment on other users as well as add their own videos on the platform. Initially developed by three PayPal employees in 2005, YouTube has gone on to rack up over 1.9 billion users worldwide.

Although YouTube is a free service, it has the option of YouTube Premium. YouTube Premium is a subscription service where users are allowed to enjoy ad-free content, as well as access to exclusive content and offline video playback.

Over the years, anyone from independent users to large corporations have used YouTube to grow their audience base further and attract new members.

In terms of generating income, YouTube and selected creators are allowed to generate advertising income from Google AdSense.

It makes sense right now to potentially jump on the YouTube bandwagon, given the massive spikes in vlogging and demands for online video content in recent times. Finding a niche that isn't already overpopulated may be a little tough, but there is potential even in the most popular markets to be a potential up and comer if you've got something different to add. Even if you are not signing up to YouTube to be a content creator, using the platform to market your current business is perfectly acceptable. Right now, YouTube is where you are most likely to find an audience to attract, as well as the best way to reach younger viewers in the market.

Starting Your Own YouTube Channel

Whether promoting your business or simply wanting to be a content creator, you will have to provide quality content for others to take notice of you. Before that, however, you will need to get the very basics right.

Determine the purpose You're going to need to know why you are creating a channel. Is it to market your business? If you're a content creator, what content do you wish to create? This will all become important later when setting up your account. For potential content creators, remember the importance of a niche and a passion.

On YouTube, you can post videos of just about anything. From video games, to political opinions, vlogs, etc. Whatever is the passion you would like to share, should be what your YouTube channel should be about. Possibly the biggest example of this is PewDiePie. Starting his YouTube channel in 2010, Felix Kjellberg, or PewDiePie, as his username suggests started his YouTube career making videos of himself playing small time indie horror games. Since then, he has gone on to become the most subscribed YouTuber from 2013 up until 2019 where he was overtaken and his channel moved into second place, however still managing to become one of the only channels to reach 100 million subscribers. It all started with a passion...

Create an account The first step you're going to need to make is to create an account. Chances are, you already have one if you have a Google account. However, if you don't set one up so that you can create your own profile on YouTube. One you have a profile, you need to create a channel on YouTube.

Spend time designing your channel, including channel art to share your personality and generate interest in your potential audience. You could choose to upload one of YouTube's templates as your channel art, or upload your own that infuses your energy and interests into the channel.

You can also choose to add a channel trailer. When someone visits our channel, your trailer will help them find out what your channel is about. This video needs to capture the attention of anyone who sees it, and entice them to check out the rest of your channel later on.

The necessary equipment You have your channel set up, but what are you going to use to make videos? At the very least, you will need the basics, which are:

A webcam. Nothing too fancy. A quality high definition webcam will do for now.

Microphone. Preferably opt for a noise canceling microphone that records the audio separately. This will help to prevent any audio discrepancies in the future.

Screen Capture. If you are planning on centering your content around video games or tutorials, you're going to need to invest in screen capture software. There are free options available, such as OBS Studio, that you can use.

Some other equipment to consider is a green screen. If you want to change your background, then you will want to consider investing in a green screen so that this is possible. If you don't have a webcam, and instead you've got a camera or a smartphone, invest in a tripod to hold it stead when you are recording.

Create content Early on, you're going to need some content that people can view on your channel. If you market a channel with no content, this will only frustrate the potential audience. To start, make a couple videos that are of quality content in your chosen niche. Around 10 should be an optimum amount to keep an audience busy in the beginning while you start to upload more content.

Promoting your channel Now that you have some content, you can promote the channel. Remember that promotion is a long term game. You will need to promote your content for a long time before you gain enough popularity to continue your growth without it. So how can you promote yourself?

Social Media. Still the beauty of the modern age. You can reach just about anyone on social media. This will give you a chance to build a small base of followers that will grow over time.

Work with other YouTubers. If you can find other YouTubers who are willing to collaborate with you, this can be a great way to pick up new audience members and expand your networks.

Forums. Forums are where most people go to have discussions and chat about things. Consider searching for a community that is relevant to your content. I would suggest being a member for a little while, and then politely suggesting that you've started a YouTube channel and would like them to check it out. This way, you can build a rapport with them first and from there, you can use this to build a greater procession of followers.

Monetization You are always going to need to find ways to increase your earning potential. Google AdSense will already be available to you, however this should just be an addition to your main source, as the revenue you will generate from AdSense will not be enough for you to have a decent passive income.

Affiliate Marketing will be one of the more popular choices to connect to your YouTube channel. If you've spent some time on YouTube, you'll see how many current YouTubers already use affiliate marketing to monetize their content.

You should also consider ***selling merchandise***. As you are now a YouTuber, you will have a lot of people who respect and enjoy the content that you make. Use this opportunity to sell merchandise that is centered around your content, which will help you turn out some substantial products, if you are successful.

Then there is the one that is becoming increasingly popular today. **Become an influencer**. If you are an influencer in a certain niche, you will start being paid to promote anything related to that niche. This can prove a healthy boost to your passive income.

Things You Need To Consider

As an independent YouTuber, you're going to be responsible for all of your own content. This means that you will have to edit your own videos to ensure they are of the best quality. If you have Windows installed, you may already have Windows Movie Maker. If not, consider cost effective alternatives that will match your needs.

You should also plan out your content before you begin. This ensures that you have a reasonable idea beforehand of what you're planning to do, and how it is relevant to your niche. Jumping straight in can leave you disorganized and lost, and you'll have wasted time on a video you most likely won't want to upload.

Pay attention to your viewers. If they leave comments on your videos, try to respond to as many as you can, to show that you are reading their comments, and that you're interested in what they have to say.

However, ignore all the negative comments. Do not engage with any form of negativity that you find. Generally, these are just others who are looking to be nasty, and it would not bode well for your image.

YouTube, overall, is a great platform to share your personality and interests with the world, while potentially generating an income. With it, you can connect with millions of like-minded people who are intrigued by your videos and your personality. Quite frankly, YouTube can be a lot of fun!

Chapter 19: Photography

Photography is one of the great many hobbies that has survived the varying advances of technology. While everyone has gained access to more high quality cameras through smartphones and other devices, there is no substitute for a good picture; taken at the right time, in the right place. I must admit that it is a hobby that I enjoy myself, although I should also admit that I'm not very good at it.

Photography gives us the opportunity to record special moments in people's lives, and allows us to share our experiences in the most meaningful ways. While many hobbies might be inaccessible to some due to a variety of reasons, photography remains an option that is accessible to us all, irrespective of our age or other demographics. Now we have the opportunity to turn that hobby into a passion!

You can use your skills to help others create memorable moments for themselves, with you providing the medium for them to cherish it for a lifetime. On top of that, you'll earn an income!

Creating Your Passive Income With Photography

So let's get started with what you will need first:

A camera.

That's it! All you need is a camera that can take high quality photos to begin with. You can even use your smartphone if it is good enough! So you've got the basics. Where do you start?

Stock photos With the term being fairly self-explanatory, you have the option to sell any stock photos you have. These can be anything from food, to a landscape to a street lamp. This is a fairly easy way to earn a little extra income contributing to the overall value. Stock photos will not make you a lot of money at all, however they don't require much work. You simply have to snap a few photos, and place it on a photography website like Shutterstock. Due to the fairly minimal work involved, adding pictures should be no fuss at all, if it can bring in any sort of income without requiring any of your time.

So if this is not going to generate the needed income, what else can you do?

Courses, Workshops and Teaching Guides A few ways you can supplement your income are with online courses and digital guides. These are considered evergreen products, as they can be sold again and again and will always be available for purchase. So once you've made them, they don't require much invest from you after you've marketed them. Workshops allow you to pass on your practical skills and techniques to those who are willing to learn so that they can better their own prospects.

Selling them as products Now this might make you feel a bit confused. However, photos can be converted and printed onto various products to be sold to the market. Consider printable merchandise such as clothing, postcards, jewelry or even large posters. This can help you determine a variety of ways in which you can potentially sell your products.

Become an affiliate Good old affiliate programs, always coming to the rescue. There are several photography companies, such as Tiny Prints, who will offer you commissions for introducing your audience to their brand.

However. You're going to need an audience.

Start a blog. Use a blog site that focuses on images, such as Tumblr to market your photography skills. Select some of your best photos for display, so that others can see the qualities you possess.

Social Media. Once again, you may want to consider more picture based social media platforms, such as Instagram and Pinterest. The main focus is to attract others to your pictures, and these sites will ensure you pull an audience to your site.

Have a website. Make sure there is a location where others can find you professionally. This can help in the future if you'd like to move on to event bookings as well during the weekends.

Develop a unique photography style. What sets your skills apart from others in the field? Find ways to show off your skills that sets you apart from the competition.

Engage with your audience. Communicate with your audience about your pictures, so that they feel that you are paying attention to them. Be considerate of the opinions they have on your art. Use the opportunity to build a community. This can help gain more traction in your audience growth as more people will want to involve themselves in this ever growing group. That will result in more people seeing your work, and more opportunities to make a profit.

Taking Your Photography Further

Now that you have an audience, a blog, a website and a social media presence, you are in the best position to ensure continuous growth in your photography income. Build your personal brand, and establish yourself as an expert in your field. This will help you in turn with your affiliates, as they will begin to gain more traction due to the increased trust and credibility your audience has placed in you.

If you feel like you've developed your personal brand, as well as your audience to a substantial level, consider approaching lectures and exhibitions to find out if they will display your work.

Out of your main working hours, offer yourself out for portrait shoots with clients and perhaps even events on weekends. While these can be a little tiring, they can be highly profitable and really boost your income further. To be hired in one of these roles, you will need to have a portfolio on your website to ensure that they can view your work.

In your free time, consider entering a few photography contests. These can provide great exposure to your work, and can help you in building connections and bring in more clients. You can also take this opportunity to try and sell your work to magazines. While this may be difficult, it will be a great boost to your reputation and your income.

Photography offers many flexible ways that you can consider to gain an income from your expertise. As a hobby and a secondary profession, it can be highly rewarding, and yet highly pleasurable at the same time.

Chapter 20: Mistakes to Avoid

In general, I've found that the theory of passive income leaves most people scratching their heads. The problem with this, is that once the idea of passive income is explained, their eyes light up with dollar signs and they assume that they are going to be wealthy with these 100% successful methods. I think that's the problem we see in a lot of things these days. People either want it all or nothing at all. However, I wonder if those same people wonder why they stay in medium income employment during the course of their lives, instead of focusing on becoming millionaires and even billionaires. It's definitely a conundrum. I suppose the real reason is fear of the unknown, or unreasonable expectations, which we will look at now. These will be the most general mistakes to avoid when you are looking to develop your own source of passive income.

The Trap of the Mind's Impulse

Strange name to give a subsection. However, it is true, isn't it? That's what happens when we make poor decisions. We react on impulse, emotion and hope, instead of on thought and objectivity. We see this all the time when it comes to passive income:

Nobody has a plan While many will roll their eyes at the thought of planning things out, when it comes to passive income you are going to need a plan to determine what it is you are planning to achieve. Without a plan, you'll lack consideration for the potential costs that may arise, and instead end up digging a hole for yourself.

The Get Rich Quick scheme My favorite. The trap that many find themselves in when they hear about passive income is the belief that passive income will generate rewards in next to no time at all. Setting unrealistic expectations will leave you feeling frustrated and discouraged, and will usually result in abandonment of the trade. Passive income is always going to be a long term game. The rewards over the long term can be substantial but you have to be prepared to be patient, and wait for, then seize opportunities.

Ignoring your assets Throughout this book, I tried to echo that although passive income does not require a lot of work in the long run, the fact is that it is still requires a degree of effort. The reality is that you're still going to have to manage these income streams as long as they are open. If you don't manage them, they may simply fall apart, and you will lose revenue by the bucketload. You need to be aware of the current state of where your income is coming from, and be prepared to act if necessary.

Unknown Finances While it may be a little harsh to say that most people make the mistake of not knowing their finances at all, the fact is that a common mistake is when income and expenses are not tracked. In the case of income, this will mean you have less of an understanding of where your business is going. Is it growing? Are you losing money? You'll have no idea if you've not tracked any income you've received. If you are not tracking your company, you may begin to feel disillusioned with your income, and let it go, even if it was showing signs of growth.

On the other hand, not keeping track of expenses can leave you without an understanding of your cash flow. In some scenarios, you could end up paying for expenses you didn't have to in the first place, however nothing was recorded, and so you ended up increasing your expenditure without knowing it. Being organized will help you in understanding the direction that your business is taking.

Ignoring the effort needed to be put in
Again, I feel the term passive income is being misconstrued. While you need to plan the development of passive income around your schedule, you do need to be consistent with it. If you are decidedly spending a full month working on your passive income, then ignoring it for another 3 months, before starting up on it again, you are merely falling behind, and each time will be like starting your business all over again. Develop a schedule for yourself, and stick to it. Be sure to modify the schedule only when it suits the needs of your business. This will ensure you are still giving your passive income a degree of priority.

Ignoring the importance of research
This is one that I feel can be mentioned for people in all walks of life. I mentioned that you

should have an invested interest in something before you decide to dedicate your time to turning it into a passive income. However, a common mistake we all make is when we believe that we know everything about a subject we are familiar with. There is always something to be learned, and if you head down this path, you could end up making several misinformed decisions along the way that could ruin your business. Always be willing to take on new information.

This should help you in avoiding some of the pitfalls that arise from the development of passive income in the future.

Conclusion

It is always a good idea to keep in your head that passive income is not a source of income that requires no work at all. The unfortunate truth is that it will require a lot of work and dedication in the beginning, but if you begin to think of the long term rewards of your initial hard work, you should be able to continue. That is why the need for passion is so important. It will drive you forward when you feel like it is no longer worth it.

Throughout this book, there have been detailed explanations on several different options to passive income. Some had limitless potential in terms of earnings. Some were very limited in how much they could achieve. However, with all options, you would be perfectly capable of receiving the equivalent of a second salary for the work you have done, provided that you actually put the work in.

It is important to remember that the potential for earnings is just that: potential. It does not mean you will earn that amount, and it certainly doesn't mean that anyone is entitled to that amount, just because they chose the field with the highest potential.

Instead, a form of income with lower potential can be infinitely more successful than one with a higher potential. This is because the practice needs to suit the individual. If it doesn't suit you, it will work against you. Choosing the practice that suits your lifestyle, personality and skills is the best way to earn the greatest profits, as the business will act as a second nature to you.

Remember throughout all of this that the key value is patience. To achieve greatness, you must be prepared to wait. And while you wait, you can learn. This will mean you are using your time valuably, and your learning will benefit the levels of greatness that you hope to achieve.

I hope that you will find the right passive income to suit your needs, and I am sure that with the right ethic, it will be a roaring success!

Good luck on your future adventures!

www.ingramcontent.com/pod-product-compliance
Lightning Source LLC
Chambersburg PA
CBHW070624220526
45466CB00001B/89